Copyright © 2011 Michael Greer
ISBN: 978-1460914700

All rights reserved. No part of this publication may be reproduced or transmitted in any form or by any means, mechanical or electronic, including photocopying and recording, or by any information storage and retrieval system, without permission in writing from the author. However, anyone may excerpt brief quotations in articles for the purpose of reviewing this publication.

While all attempts have been made to verify information provided in this publication, the author assumes no responsibility for errors, omissions, or contrary interpretation of the subject matter herein. The author wants to emphasize that the information contained herein may not be in accordance with various recommended practices within specific organizations. The material represents the author's preferred practices and processes based on the author's professional experience in various organizations and industries.

The author assumes no responsibility or liability whatsoever on the behalf of any purchaser or reader of these materials. Any perceived slights of specific people or organizations are unintentional.

Michael Greer
http://michaelgreer.biz

NOTE: At the time of this printing, this book is **also available in Kindle, NOOK, and PDF formats.** Updated information about the latest versions (and many related links to free videos, podcast, evolving tool collections and more) can be found at this URL:
http://michaelgreer.biz/?page_id=636

Table of Contents

DEDICATION 4

ACKNOWLEDGEMENTS 4

INTRODUCTION 5

PM MINIMALIST VALUES: A FRAMEWORK FOR RETHINKING PM 6

OVERVIEW 7

QUICK START CHECKLIST: THE ABSOLUTE LEAST YOU CAN DO! 8

THE NUTS AND BOLTS: 10 STEPS TO PROJECT SUCCESS 9

STEP 1: DEFINE THE PROJECT CONCEPT, THEN GET SUPPORT AND APPROVAL 10

    Worksheet: The Project Charter

STEP 2: GET YOUR TEAM TOGETHER AND START THE PROJECT. 13

    Sample Responsibility/Accountability Matrix
    Responsibility/Accountability Matrix Worksheet

STEP 3: FIGURE OUT EXACTLY WHAT THE FINISHED WORK PRODUCTS WILL BE. 16

    Example: Phased Work Breakdown Structure
    Worksheet: Project Scope Statement

STEP 4: FIGURE OUT WHAT YOU NEED TO DO TO COMPLETE THE WORK PRODUCTS. (IDENTIFY TASKS AND PHASES.) 20

    Sample Network Diagram

STEP 5: ESTIMATE TIME, EFFORT, AND RESOURCES. 24

    Sample Effort/Duration Table.
    Template: Effort/Duration Table.

STEP 6: BUILD A SCHEDULE. 28

    Sample Project Schedules

STEP 7: ESTIMATE THE COSTS. 33

    Sample Cost Estimation Worksheet

STEP 8: KEEP THE PROJECT MOVING. 36

    Checklist: Keep the Project Moving
    Worksheet: The Project Status Report
    Worksheet: Project Communications Planner

STEP 9: HANDLE SCOPE CHANGES. 42

    Worksheet: Project Scope Change Order

STEP 10: CLOSE OUT PHASES, CLOSE OUT THE PROJECT. 45

    Worksheet: Sign-Off Form [For a Project Phase]
    Worksheet: Project Sign-Off Form [For an Entire Project]
    Project "Post Mortem" Review Questions

THE PEOPLE STUFF: 10 SETS OF CHALLENGES TO INSPIRE TEAMS ... 54
- THE 10 SETS OF CHALLENGES ... 55
- TRUST YOUR JUDGMENT ... 56
- LET GO OF PERFECTIONISM ... 61
- CELEBRATE THE CHAOS WITHIN ... 63
- EMBRACE THE WORK ITSELF ... 65
- TAKE THE RISK ... 67
- JUST SAY NO ... 72
- LISTEN, UNDERSTAND, COLLABORATE ... 76
- JUST DO IT! ... 78
- CONSCIOUSLY CHOOSE YOUR ATTITUDE ... 83
- BE THE CHANGE YOU WANT TO SEE ... 90

TAKING CARE OF YOURSELF: MANAGING YOUR PRIORITIES, TIME, & ENERGY ... 94
- BACK TO BASICS: MANAGE YOUR ENERGY ... 95
- LEVERAGE YOUR SIGNATURE STRENGTHS ... 97
- MANAGE YOUR TIME ... 98
- UNDERSTAND AND MANAGE YOUR STRESS ... 104
- SUMMARY ... 110
- LEARN MORE ... 111

* GLOSSARY OF TERMS USED ... 112

PM MINIMALIST VALUES EXPLAINED ... 113

THE PM MINIMALIST INTEGRATION GUIDE: ADOPTING PROJECT MANAGEMENT MINIMALISM IN YOUR ORGANIZATION ... 116

Dedication

This book is dedicated to all the clients who in the last 25 years or so have invited me into their organizations to teach my customized project management (PM) basics workshops. **From them I learned this key lesson which every "PM expert" needs to know: Enough is enough... especially when you're talking PM!**

Every once in a while, when I rolled out my big collection of cosmic and sometimes complex PM tools and processes, there were people in the group who "pushed back" with their common sense and proved to me that **leaner is always better!** As the years have gone by, I have become convinced that **there are really just a handful of important PM tools, artifacts, and processes that matter** -- and that many of the more esoteric procedures that the PM consultants and experts push at PM newbies are more trouble than they're worth!

So to you, my courageous and sometimes cantankerous clients, I truly owe my gratitude. You helped me cut through the heaps of PM jargon and esoterica and find the essences of true PM minimalism. I hope this little book accurately reflects the lessons you have taught me.

Acknowledgements

Many of the tools in this e-book originally appeared in my **HRD Press** book, *The Project Manager's Partner, 2nd edition (2001)*. In fact, that book contains over 57 tools, guidelines, and worksheets for project managers.

I'd like to acknowledge the effort of all those at HRD Press who helped me build and who currently sell and distribute the Partner. It is a most comprehensive collection of PM tools and processes. And I am proud to have created it. The PM minimalist approach advocated here would simply not have been possible without my earlier work on the Partner. For more information about the Partner, see this page at my website:
- **The Project Manager's Partner, 2nd Edition** -- http://michaelgreer.biz/?p=208

The third part of this book owes its existence to the inspiration of **Brian Johnson**, the creator of **PhilosophersNotes**. After many months of listening to Brian's 20-minute audio distillations of "The Biggest Ideas from 100 of The Most Influential Books On Personal Growth" I was transformed. And I began my quest to "pay forward" Brian's gifts to me by attempting to share similar wisdom in the realm of project management. This led to my **Inspired Project Teams** blog and podcasts, 10 of which make up the second part of this book. Brian's genius, and more importantly his infectious enthusiasm for all things that are growth-oriented, should be experienced by everyone! So go to **PhilosophersNotes** and "get your wisdom on!" (http://www.philosophersnotes.com/)

> *Michael Greer*

Introduction

"Who you jivin' with that cosmic debris?" – Frank Zappa

Project management (PM) is not rocket science! And, despite what many PM "experts" would like you to believe, it's fairly easy for anyone to learn to use a few basic PM tools and processes to assure that projects are well-organized and completed on time, on budget, and with excellent results.

Unfortunately, a vast army of consultants and writers, encouraged by professional associations and their certifying bodies, have puffed up the practice of PM so that it appears to be much more complex than it really is. But just think about it! Every day millions of people all over the world work on do-it-yourself home improvement projects, organize events for their local community service groups, complete work-related projects assigned by their supervisors, and so on. And the vast majority of these people have likely had no formal PM training. Yet somehow they get results using only their common sense and specific knowledge of the problem they are trying to solve. So **a strong case can be made that extensive PM training and certification is a "nice to have," not a "need to have."**

On the other hand, I know that when smart people who have had no formal PM training are given a few key PM tools and coaching, they really thrive. In several decades of teaching PM Basics to professionals in many different fields I've learned that **when a PM newbie combines deep knowledge of her profession with a few simple PM tools and techniques, amazing things begin to happen!** Her unique intuition and judgment, merged with a little PM discipline, can produce robust project plans and powerful PM results.

My purpose here is to cut through the jungle of broad PM theory and sometimes-arcane PM practices and help you acquire "just enough" PM discipline to get good results in your projects – without heaping on a bunch of burdensome PM stuff that can bury your projects in administrivia and smother the joy out of them.

I hope you find this book to be useful. And I hope that you carefully, assertively pick and choose from it "just enough" PM tools to help you thrive in your role as project manager.

> ➢ MG

PM Minimalist Values: A Framework for Rethinking PM

"Any intelligent fool can make things bigger, more complex, and more violent. It takes a touch of genius – and a lot of courage – to move in the opposite direction." – E.F. Schumacher

"Besides the noble art of getting things done, there is the noble art of leaving things undone. The wisdom of life consists in the elimination of non-essentials". – Lin Yutang

"Simplicity is the ultimate sophistication." – Leonardo DaVinci

"Everything should be made as simple as possible, but not simpler." – Albert Einstein

---

Project Management (PM) Minimalism **is the practice of doing "just enough" PM to get the job done, and no more.**

The PM Minimalist Values summarized below may be applied to any project in any industry or professional practice.

Practicing PM Minimalism takes courage and judgment! You're going to have to decide what "just enough" PM is for your particular project. Later in this e-book you'll find plenty of lean, simple, and professional-level PM tools and guidelines. And when applied to most projects, these tools and guidelines prove to be quite valuable. But remember:

> **You should reject or ignore any PM tools or recommended practices that won't help your project team or that make your project too complex or bloated.**

The PM Minimalist Values[++]

Use these Values to help you decide what constitutes "just enough" PM for your project.

- Create fewer deliverables with fewer features.
- Do less work.
- Absorb or neutralize (but don't ignore) anyone who can reject or rethink your deliverables.
- Work as fast as quality permits – maybe faster!
- Deliver something – anything – as soon as possible.
- "Make it real" as often as possible with models, mock-ups, prototypes, & samples.
- Revise or reject something as soon as possible.
- Give up on the project earlier; cut your losses.
- Ignore external-to-the-project "professionals" who would have you puff up the project or its work processes.
- Enjoy creating; don't put up with simply slogging through.

[++] *(For a full explanation of each of these values,* ***see "PM Minimalist Values Explained"*** *at the end of this book.)*

Overview

This book is organized into four main parts.

Quick Start Checklist: The Absolute Least You Can Do!

- A one-page checklist, lean and to-the-point.
- ***Start with this to organize and manage your first project. You may not need anything else!***

The Nuts and Bolts: 10 Steps to Project Success

This part of the book provides tools to help you perform these essential PM steps:

- Step 1: Define the project concept, then get support and approval.
- Step 2: Get your team together and start the project.
- Step 3: Figure out exactly what the finished work products will be.
- Step 4: Figure out what you need to do to complete the work products. (Identify tasks and phases.)
- Step 5: Estimate time, effort, and resources.
- Step 6: Build a schedule.
- Step 7: Estimate the costs.
- Step 8: Keep the project moving.
- Step 9: Handle scope changes.
- Step 10: Close out phases, close out the project.

The People Stuff: 10 Sets of Challenges to Inspire Project Teams

This part will help you inspire and motivate your project team. It provides inspirational quotes, thoughts, and specific challenges for you and your team. Here are the topics:

- Trust Your Judgment
- Let Go of Perfectionism
- Celebrate the Chaos Within
- Embrace the Work Itself
- Take the Risk
- Just Say No
- Listen, Understand, Collaborate
- Just Do It!
- Consciously Choose Your Attitude
- Be the Change You Want to See

Taking Care of Yourself: Managing Your Priorities, Time & Energy

This part of the book gets personal. It provides a bit of a pep talk and some specific guidelines to help you manage your priorities, time and energy. Broad topics include:

- Back to Basics: Manage Your Energy
- Leverage Your Signature Strengths
- Manage Your Time
- Understand and Manage Your Stress

Quick Start Checklist: The Absolute Least You Can Do!

Get your project rolling quickly, with Minimum effort, by doing these Minimum chores. If you want to expand any of these chores or get more information about them, see the suggested Step in "The Nuts and Bolts..." section of this e-book.

- ❏ **Mini-Charter:** Write a one paragraph description of your project's tangible finished product. Get this reviewed & approved by your boss or customer.
    (See Step 1: Define the project concept, then get support and approval.)

- ❏ **Team:** Get together everyone who'll help build the finished product, who'll use it, or who might cause trouble or force it to be changed if they don't like it.
    (See Step 2: Get your team together and start the project.)

- ❏ **Go wide**: Working as a team, brainstorm to create a "wide view" list of "wished for" deliverables. (Pretend you could build anything on this list.)
    (See Step 3: Figure out exactly what the finished work products will be.)

- ❏ **Slash & Burn:** Working as a team, divide the "wide view" list of deliverables into three equal-sized lists: 1) Those we "must build," 2) Those we "could build," and 3) Those we "can wait to build."
    (See Step 3: Figure out exactly what the finished work products will be.)

- ❏ **The To-Do/Assignment List:** Working as a team, list the tasks required to create the "must build" items and assign these tasks to specific people.
    (See Step 4: Figure out what to do…& Step 2 [Responsibility/Acct. Matrix].)

- ❏ **The Schedule:** Still working as a team, make your "best guess" about how long it will take to complete each task. Then, referring to a calendar, make a schedule. Include each task, specific deadlines, dates, and the names of people assigned to each task. (**CAUTION**: *If your project schedule exceeds 1 month, try to break it into a series of smaller projects. Smaller projects are more likely to succeed.*)
    (See Step 5: Estimate time, effort, resources & Step 6: Build a schedule.)

- ❏ **Get started**: Do the tasks as described in the schedule.
    (See Steps 8: Keep … moving, 9: Handle scope changes, & 10: Close out...)

- ❏ **Inspect and correct**: While the project is under way, find out:
    - ❏ Are "must build" items on time?
    - ❏ Are "must build" items of high enough quality?
    - ❏ Is everyone doing what they promised?
    - ❏ Do people need more help or need to have obstacles removed?
    - ❏ What must we correct or change to finish the project on time?
        (See Steps 8: Keep … moving, 9: Handle scope changes, & 10: Close out...)

- ❏ **Post Mortem & Lessons Learned:** When the project is over, look back & figure out how you could have improved it. List Lessons Learned, then use them to make you next project better.
    (See Step 10: Close out phases, close out the project.)

Did the above PM process & tools work OK? If not, adjust for your next project by: 1) dropping some chores, or 2) changing/adding some processes or tools.

The Project Management Minimalist: Just Enough PM to Rock Your Projects!

The Nuts and Bolts: 10 Steps to Project Success

In this part of the book, we introduce important PM tools and practices that will help you get results by completing each of the 10 Steps to Project Success.

Each Step is divided into these sections:

- **Overview** – An introduction to what's going on in the Step.
- **Results** – The end product of the Step.
- **Process** – The specific actions to take to complete the Step.
- **The Minimalist Squeeze** – After you've worked the process for this Step, make a final pass and give it a "Minimalist Squeeze" to shrink it as much as possible.
- **Tool, Worksheet, Guidelines, Samples, etc.** – Things you can use to help you complete the step and get top-quality results.

Step 1: Define the project concept, then get support and approval.

Overview

In this step you need to **define the project concept clearly enough so that you can get support from key people in your organization.** You do not need to come up with a detailed plan at this point. But you do need to get preliminary (and formal) support for the project.

In sales terms, you are "qualifying the buyer," then trying to close the sale. That is, you are testing the waters with a preliminary, broad-brush description of the project so that you can:
- Find out if anyone else is likely to support your work or is willing to help you do the work.
- Obtain a project champion or sponsor.
- Find a source (or several sources) of project resources (such as people, equipment, and money) needed to help you complete the project.
- Get your project formally approved and funded.

Results

This Step should result in the following:
- A series of conversations, brainstorming sessions, and other formal or informal discussions about the project concept with your supervisor and key people whom you hope will provide project support
- An approved Project Charter

Process

1. Figure out if the project is needed. That is, find out if it supports a:
    - Market demand
    - Business or strategic initiative
    - Customer request
    - Technological advance
    - Legal requirement
    - Other important organizational initiative

2. Create a Project Charter that:
    - Formally recognizes the existence of the project
    - Is supported by a manager external to the project and at a high enough organizational level to support project needs (i.e., a sponsor* who can help the project team acquire the resources* they need – people, equipment, facilities, funding, etc.)
    - Authorizes the project manager to apply organizational resources (people, equipment, materials) to project activities

3. Get the Project Charter approved (physically signed) by a project sponsor.

Note: If you can't get your Charter formally approved, then you should abandon the project -- plain and simple. In fact, in many organizations the Charter is established as a formal "approval gate" which allows senior managers to sort out and eliminate lower-priority projects. This sorting process not only saves the organization money by focusing energy only on high-priority projects, but it can help prevent the burn-out that results when people are assigned to too many projects or when people find themselves "swimming upstream" on projects that aren't really valuable enough to win the support they need to succeed

The Minimalist Squeeze

1. Got your Project Charter approved? Great! Now, without consulting your sponsor, give it a quick review and ask yourself:
    - What's the smallest chunk of this project we might be able to complete easily in the next two weeks? ... the next month?
2. Resolve that when you get your team together in Step 2, you will ask them to help you design your project as a collection of short, doable mini-projects, beginning with that first chunk you identified above.
3. Make some notes so you can share your "small chunk" ideas with the team.
4. Benefits of small projects:
    - Planning is more accurate when you are looking ahead only a few weeks.
    - Allows you to "change your mind" without such dire consequences.
    - Opportunity to fail sooner means less is lost (fewer labor hours, fewer dollars, fewer "heart" and team effort.)
    - Allows the team to "come up for air" and get closure more often instead of spending month on end in the trenches laboring toward a distant goal.
    - Allows frequent celebrations of milestones (keeping the team motivated).

---

* The asterisk (*) beside this (or any) PM term means that you will find a full definition of it in the "*Glossary of Terms Used" at the end of this book.

Worksheet: The Project Charter

Project Name: _____ **Date:** _____
Project Manager: _____
Project Tracking Number: _____

Project Justification (problem or opportunity addressed):

Overview of Deliverables (high-level, broad-brush only—provide details, if any, in appendices**):

Specific Project Objectives & Success Criteria (schedule, cost, quality):

Primary Stakeholders & Roles (including broad statement of roles and responsibilities of all customers, sponsors, contributors, reviewers, managers, sign-off authorities, project manager, etc.):

Key Assumptions (including broad statement of sponsor/stakeholder inputs and resources to be provided, as well as a delineation of "what's outside" project scope):

Signatures—The following people agree that the above information is accurate:
- Project team members:

- Project sponsor and/or authorizing manager(s):

** Appendices (Needs Analysis/Feasibility Study Notes, Detailed Work Breakdown Structure, Preliminary Schedule, Preliminary Cost Estimate, Sample Deliverables, Background Memos/Reports, Organization Chart of Project Team, others as needed).

[This tool is from The Project Manager's Partner, 2nd Edition, © Copyright 2001, Michael Greer/HRD Press]

Step 2: Get your team together and start the project.

Overview
Here's your challenge in this Step: Find all the people who will care about (and use) the project outcomes or who can help you create the project outcomes. Then get these people organized as a team. Broadly speaking, these people are called project stakeholders*.

In Step 1, we obtained formal support and approval for our project. So now we can justify the effort required to locate core project team members (people who will work to produce specific project deliverables*) and locate all other stakeholders (people whose interests will be affected by the project outcomes) and organize all of these people as a team. When we've assembled this team, we can run a Kickoff Meeting and get started.

Caution: If you don't involve all stakeholders in an active and engaged fashion from the beginning, you are likely to suffer the consequences of rework* when they finally figure out what you and your project team are up to…. and they then take action to leave their mark on it! So, if you want to avoid the penalties of rework (i.e., avoid schedule overruns and blown budgets), take great care to identify and get all stakeholders involved.

Results
This Step should result in the following:
- A series of conversations, brainstorming sessions, and other formal/informal discussions about the project concept with all stakeholders
- Commitments from stakeholders to play particular roles on the project team throughout or at specific times in the project.
- Written documentation that captures roles and responsibilities of all stakeholders
- A Kickoff Meeting that orients all project team members to their roles and responsibilities and gets the project started (See #5, below, for details.)

Process
1. Examine the Project Charter and make a list of everyone whose interests will be affected by the project or who will help create the project outcomes.
2. Examine any local organization charts, customer organization charts, and lists of related agencies, etc., and then expand the list you made in Item 1 (above).
3. Talk to senior people whose names appear on your list of stakeholders and begin to figure out the key project roles and responsibilities, reporting relationships, etc.
4. Complete a Responsibility/Accountability Matrix (See sample on next page.)
5. Plan and run a **Kickoff Meeting that meets these objectives**:
   - Clarify "broad brush" work products (deliverables*).
   - Clarify roles and responsibilities of team members.
   - Create a shared sense of purpose among team members.
   - Obtain specific commitment of each team member to complete assigned tasks according to schedule and budget constraints.
   - Make sure all team members have what they need to start work.

The Minimalist Squeeze
Use the Minimalist approach to build your project team:
1. Create a "just large enough" core team (people who will create outputs and be your primary experts/workers) to complete the work efficiently and to ensure high quality results.
2. Use these Minimalist Value to help you figure out how many external reviewers and non-core people you need:
    - Absorb or neutralize (but don't ignore) anyone who can reject or rethink your deliverables.
    - Ignore external-to-the-project "professionals" who would have you puff up the project or its work processes.

The Responsibility/Accountability Matrix

Below is a sample Responsibility/Accountability Matrix. You can change it to suit your project. The main idea is to use it to capture all of your team's agreements about who will do what on your project team.

Sample Responsibility/Accountability Matrix

RESPONSIBILITY/ACCOUNTABILITY MATRIX

Phase ↘ / *Person* →	Bill	Charmaine	Juan	Leticia	Mary
Determine Need and Feasibility	A	S	P	P	P
Create Project Plan	A	S, I	I	I	I
Create Deliverables Specifications	A, P	S	R	P	P
Create Deliverables	A, P	S	P	P	P
Test and Implement	A	I	R	R	P

P = Participate A = Accountable R = Review I = Input Required S = Sign-off Required

(For your convenience, there is a blank Responsibility/Accountability matrix on the next page.)

[Sample is from The Project Manager's Partner, 2nd Edition, © Copyright 2001, Michael Greer/HRD Press]

Responsibility/Accountability Matrix

Task/Phase * ↓	Person →						

P = Participate   A = Accountable   R = Review Required   I = Input Required   S = Sign-off

This column might also be labeled "activities" or "deliverables."

[This tool is from The Project Manager's Partner, 2nd Edition, © Copyright 2001, Michael Greer/HRD Press]

Step 3: Figure out exactly what the finished work products will be.

Overview

Here's the deal: **You can't manage what you can't see.** So the goal in Step 3 is to figure out exactly what specific items (i.e., tangible work products, also called deliverables*) the project team must create. In a nutshell, you need to meet with all of your stakeholders and conduct a brainstorming session in order to **document, in "high resolution," everything you are going to be building.** And it's best to do this as a team, in order to avoid conflicting interpretations of deliverables later as they are being created.

In this way, your team expands your initial Project Charter to create a more comprehensive Scope Statement.

Results

- A series of conversations, brainstorming sessions, and other formal/informal discussions about specific project deliverables*
- A Work Breakdown Structure (WBS) in rough form as created by a brainstorming group (i.e., a bunch of yellow stickies spread out all over a wall, a collection of flip chart pages scribbled with items, a rough "mind map," etc.)
- A polished WBS which clearly lists 1) all interim deliverables that the end user will not see (such as scripts, flow charts, outlines, etc.) and 2) all finished deliverables that will be turned over to the user when the project is completed. [See Example Phased Work Breakdown Structure below.]
- A Project Scope Statement that expands the Project Charter to include the WBS and other items identified by the team in brainstorming sessions [See Worksheet: Project Scope Statement below.]
- Approval of the Project Scope Statement and WBS by the sponsor and appropriate stakeholders.

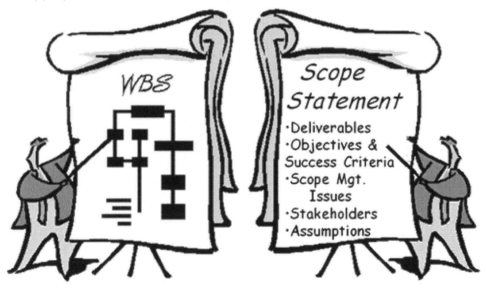

Process

1. Assemble all project documentation, including the Charter, technical specifications, proposals, descriptions of related strategic initiatives, and so on.
2. Assemble the project team, including as many stakeholders as possible.
3. Conduct a brainstorming session in which the stakeholders create a rough draft of the WBS.
4. Polish and finalize the WBS.
5. Expand the Project Charter and transform it into a formal Project Scope Statement.
6. Circulate the WBS and Project Scope Statement to appropriate stakeholders/sponsors and get formal approval.

The Minimalist Squeeze

After you've "gone wide" and created a comprehensive wish list of deliverables, apply "Scope Triage" to reduce the number of deliverables:

1. Look at your comprehensive list of deliverables or WBS.
2. Divide these into *three equal collections*: **Must Do, Should Do, and Could Do.** (For example, if you have identified 15 deliverables, you must place 5 of your deliverables in each collection.)

3. As you work through the next Steps, plan to complete only the "Must Do" deliverables. (You can return to the Should and Could do items later, in your next project, if you decide they are really needed.)
4. Use this Minimalist Value to guide your thinking:
   - Create fewer deliverables with fewer features.
   (Because every deliverable, every feature shoots out tendrils and roots all through your project and will chew up time and effort as your team works to define it, create it, revise it, & finalize it! Yikes! Be careful what you wish for!)

(Note: I first learned of the "Scope Triage" concept from Ted Marcus' online article, "Scope Containment in Information System Projects." Sorry... I can't find any current citations or URLs for this. In any case: Thanks, Ted!)

Example: Phased Work Breakdown Structure

Below is an example of a phased work breakdown structure (WBS). The team responsible for Project X has identified five different phases into which they might cluster all of their various project deliverables: Need & Feasibility, Project Plan, Deliverables Specifications, Deliverables, and Testing and Implementation. Within each of these phases we can see many *finished deliverables* (such as prototypes, approved deliverables, etc.) and also many *interim deliverables* (such as the project charter, flowcharts, reviews, revisions, formal approvals, test strategies, etc.).

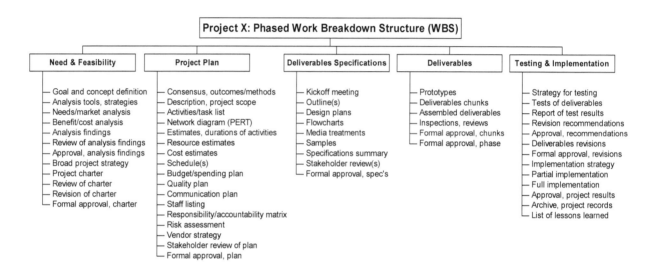

Note: In this example of a work breakdown chart (WBS), all of the items are expressed as *nouns*. As such, they are measurable, tangible targets or work products that the team must create to complete the project. **Don't use verbs or try to make a list of tasks** at this point. Simply capture a list of tangible work products. Later, in Step 4, we'll focus on tasks.

[This tool is from The Project Manager's Partner, 2nd Edition, © Copyright 2001, Michael Greer/HRD Press]

The Project Management Minimalist: Just Enough PM to Rock Your Projects!

Worksheet: Project Scope Statement

Project Name: _____   **Date:** _____
Project Manager: _____
Project Tracking Number: _____

Project Justification (problem or opportunity addressed):

Overview of Deliverables (. . . broad brush only—Place detailed WBS in appendices**):

Specific Project Objectives & Success Criteria (schedule, cost, quality):

Scope Management Issues (including ways scope changes will be handled, what kinds of things are definitely *outside* the scope of this project, etc.):

Primary Stakeholders & Roles (including broad statement of roles and responsibilities of all customers, sponsors, contributors, reviewers, managers, sign-off authorities, project manager, etc.):

Key Assumptions (including broad statement of sponsor/stakeholder inputs and resources to be provided, as well as what tasks and deliverables lie *outside* the project scope):

Signatures—The following people agree that the above information is accurate:
- Project team members:

- Project sponsor and/or authorizing manager(s):

** Appendices (Needs Analysis/Feasibility Study Notes, Detailed Work Breakdown Structure, Preliminary Schedule, Preliminary Cost Estimate, Sample Deliverables, Background Memos/Reports, Organization Chart of Project Team, others as needed).

[This tool is from The Project Manager's Partner, 2nd Edition, © Copyright 2001, Michael Greer/HRD Press]

Step 4: Figure out what you need to do to complete the work products. (Identify tasks and phases.)

Overview

In Step 3 you made a list of all the items (deliverables*) that the project team must create in order to complete the project. In this Step you need to figure out exactly what tasks your team will be performing to create each of these items. In other words, you must **make a giant "to do" list of all project tasks.** Finally, you must **organize this giant "to do" list into** easy-to-comprehend chunks called **phases*.**

Results

- A list or graphical collection of all project tasks that must be completed to create project deliverables.
- A network diagram showing the sequence and flow of all project tasks, including opportunities for stakeholders to review and approve deliverables as they evolve
- Descriptions or illustrations of project phases

Process

1. Assemble all project documentation, including the stakeholder-approved Project Scope Statement, WBS, technical specifications, proposals, and so on.
2. Assemble the core project team and as many stakeholders as possible.
3. Conduct a brainstorming session in which the core project team and stakeholders do the following:
    a. Examine each specific deliverable that must be created. (Refer to your WBS from Step 3.)
    b. List the specific tasks that must be performed to cause that particular deliverable to evolve from rough idea to finished product. (Use yellow stickies, flip charts, white boards, mind mapping methodology and any other brainstorming tools you like.)
    c. Incorporate plenty of opportunities for stakeholders to review work products in small increments, as they are evolving. So, for example, if you are writing a report, don't wait until you're finished to share it with reviewers. Instead, share (and get feedback and make revisions to) an outline first and then a rough draft, before you spend your time finalizing and polishing the report.

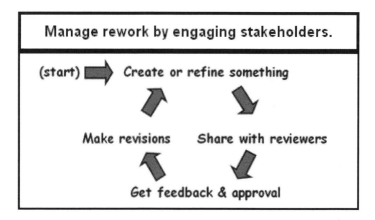

Specifically, insert as many "create, share, feedback, revise" cycles into your task list as possible. This will help prevent unplanned rework (and blown schedules from having stakeholders reject your deliverables!) by building opportunities into your plan for review and revision.
- d. Combine and organize the list of tasks/activities into broad collections of related tasks or phases.*
- e. Create a network diagram (flow chart) showing the sequence and flow of all project tasks, activities, and phases. (See Sample Network Diagram, below.)
4. Polish and finalize the network diagram and task list.
5. Circulate the network diagram and task list to appropriate stakeholders/sponsor and get formal approval (i.e., sign-off).

Note: Recent PM Innovations Emphasize Smaller Projects, Shorter Iterations

In recent years several formal PM methodologies have emerged to deal with the challenge of getting new products to market faster. PM geeks, especially those in the IT world, are likely to talk to you about one or more of the following techniques:
- Agile PM
- Extreme Programming (XP)
- Scrum PM
- Some arcane outgrowth or combination of these.

All of these processes share some common themes:
- Build small, lean collections of deliverables.
- Organize projects to fit within relatively short periods of time. (Entire projects may take less than a month. And many proponents suggest keeping projects within two-week time frames.)
- Create many iterations of deliverables.
- Circulate these iterations quickly so that they may be reviewed and/or tested, then revised, as soon as possible.
- Keep the PM controls loose; encourage decision-making and approval authority to move as far down the organizational ladder as possible. (Empower teams.)

The bad news: Advocates of these processes sometimes have the "born again" energy of any convert to a new belief. And they can be fairly pushy about requiring you to swear to (and practice) the dogma of their new PM religion. Worse, they have their own catechism, made up of some fairly arcane terminology. And they tend to be impatient if you don't speak this language.

The good news: *These new PM methodologies are not all that different from what we advocate here in the PM Minimalist approach. At their essence, each has some version of the "create, share, get feedback, revise" cycle shown in the graphic above.* Better yet, there are many good Wikipedia articles (some with pictures!) that can quickly orient you to any of these approaches. So you can easily get yourself up to speed and ready to work with their proponents.

The bottom line: Don't let these guys baffle you with B.S. If you practice PM Minimalism as outlined in our 10 Steps, you are fairly well prepared to translate your PM into any of these methodologies.

The Minimalist Squeeze

After you've listed as many tasks, phases, and to-dos as possible, use the Minimalist approach to streamline and shape the list:

1. Create a "just large enough" list of tasks, etc. to complete the work efficiently and to ensure high quality results. Balance these:
   - Enough stakeholder reviews to help avoid rework, but not so many that you "puff up" the project.
   - Enough "fingers in the pie" (shared tasks) to ensure quality/cross checking, but not so many as to get in each other's' way and waste time.
2. Use these Minimalist Values to guide you here:
   - Do less work.
   - Deliver something – anything – as soon as possible.
   - "Make it real" as often as possible with models, mock-ups, prototypes, & samples.
   - Revise or reject something as soon as possible.
   - Ignore external-to-the-project "professionals" who would have you puff up the project or its work processes.

Sample Network Diagram

Below is a sample of a completed network diagram. Notice that it shows four key elements:
- Phases
- Tasks
- Stakeholder/sponsor review points
- Stakeholder/sponsor closure (approval or sign-off) points

Because projects* are, by definition, temporary endeavors, it is essential to identify how each phase or collection of activities will be judged by stakeholders to be formally or officially completed. So the review and approval points (indicated by check marks) are essential to ensure that the project deliverables move toward closure and completion. Without including specific tasks that call for review and approval points, project deliverables might never be formally judged to be completed!

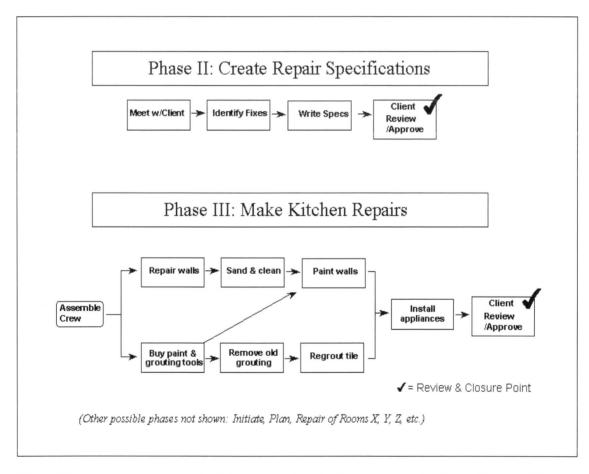

Note: When you create your task list and network diagram, you don't need to specify exactly who will be performing each of the tasks. You are probably not ready to make specific job assignments at this point. So simply focus on the tasks that need to be performed. In the next Step, you can review this task list and figure out who will be doing what.

Step 5: Estimate time, effort, and resources.

Overview

After you have identified the project tasks to be performed, you need to figure out how long it will take to complete each task. To do this, you need to **look at each task in your task list or network diagram and think about three things:**

- **Resources** – Any people, equipment, and materials needed to complete the task
- **Effort** – the number of labor units (staff hours, person-days, or -weeks) required to complete the task
- **Duration** – the period of time over which the task takes place

Sometimes new project managers confuse duration and effort. Here's an analogy to illustrate the difference between the two: Let's say you are putting in a new sidewalk. You have two workers digging out the old cement and then pouring new cement. The workers will expend the effort of one 8-hour work day to complete their digging and pouring of cement. So two workers X 8 hours = 16 hours of effort. After these workers complete their one day of work, the cement will require 3 more days to properly dry and cure before it can be used. So the duration (period of time consumed) of the project is 1 day of work by the workers + 3 days of time spent by cement drying and curing = 4 days duration total.

When you review your task list and capture information about the resources, effort, and duration required to complete each task, you are laying the groundwork for building these important project specifications later:

- **Schedule** – Your project calendar is derived from your estimates of duration.
- **Labor requests and labor assignments** – Your requests for numbers of workers and the time you will need them to work are derived from your estimates of effort.
- **Cost estimates** – Since labor costs typically make up the largest part of any project's costs, your accurate estimates of effort required by workers are essential to estimating accurate overall project costs.

Results

- A detailed estimate of the duration, effort, and resources required to complete each project task.
- A summary of duration, effort, and resources required for the entire project

Process

1. Assemble all project documentation, including the approved Project Scope Statement, WBS, network diagram, task lists, technical specifications, proposals, and so on. And if the work of anyone on your team is subject to union or government regulations, you should have these policies available as reference.
2. Assemble the core project team and as many stakeholders as possible. (If the core project team members and stakeholders have never worked on the type of tasks listed in this project, try to find people who have had actual experience successfully completing these types of tasks. You'll need to ask these people for

guidance about what kinds and how many resources might be needed and how much time you should allow for each of these resources to complete their tasks.)
3. Conduct a brainstorming session in which the core project team and stakeholders do the following:
    a. Examine each specific task that must be completed. (See network diagram or completed task list from Step 4.)
    b. List the specific duration, effort, and resources required to complete each project task. (See the Sample Effort/Duration Table below.)
    c. Create a summary of duration, effort, and resources required for the entire project.
4. Circulate the summary of duration, effort, and resources required to appropriate stakeholders/sponsor and get formal approval.

The Minimalist Squeeze

Use the Minimalist approach to refine your estimate of time, effort, and resources:
1. Find at all the tasks that are shared by two or more people.
2. Challenge the assumption that they must be shared. (Task sharing often adds time for communications, arguing, etc. among those sharing a task.) Ask: How might we adjust these tasks so that they can be done by one person?
3. Find all the durations that have been extended by "down time" or waiting for someone to review and respond with feedback. Can these time periods be reduced? (For example, can we get reviewer's to get us their feedback sooner?)
4. Can we adjust what we're delivering so it can be completed more quickly? (For example, might we deliver and use a draft or prototype instead of a more highly polished item.)
5. Use these Minimalist Values to guide you here:
    - Work as fast as quality permits – maybe faster!
    - Deliver something – anything – as soon as possible.
    - Ignore external-to-the-project "professionals" who would have you puff up the project or its work processes.
    - Do less work.

Sample Effort/Duration Table

Below is an Effort/Duration table for a small writing project. Note that **this table shows:**
- All tasks to be completed
- All resources assigned to tasks
- The effort/hours needed of each resource for the whole project (These will later help us make requests for resources, make specific job assignments, and estimate costs.)
- The durations of each task and of the entire project. (Later, in Step 6, these will help us create a project schedule.)

Phase, Activity, or Task:	*Resource:* Writer *Effort:*	*Resource:* Technical SME *Effort:*	*Resource:* Client Reviewer *Effort:*	*Resource:* Research Computer *Effort:*	**Duration:**
Discuss requirements	1 hour	1 hour	1 hour	—	1 hour
Develop outline	8 hours	3 hours	—	4 hours	8 hours
Review outline	—	—	1 hour	—	8 hours
Obtain client feedback & approval	1 hour	1 hour	1 hour	—	1 hour
Write 1st draft	24 hours	8 hours	—	2 hours	24 hours
Review draft	—	—	3 hours	—	40 hours
Obtain client feedback & approval	3 hours	3 hours	3 hours	—	3 hours
Revise & finalize	6 hours	1 hour	—	1 hour	6 hours
Totals:	43 hours	17 hours	9 hours	7 hours	91 hours

[Example from The Project Manager's Partner, 2nd Edition, © Copyright 2001, Michael Greer/HRD Press]

Template: Effort/Duration Table

Phase, Activity, or Task:	Resource: _____ Effort:	Resource: _____ Effort:	Resource: _____ Effort:	Resource: _____ Effort:	Duration:
Totals:					

[This tool is from The Project Manager's Partner, 2nd Edition, © Copyright 2001, Michael Greer/HRD Press]

NOTE: Is all this "guessing" at effort/duration a little scary? Do you feel like you're just "making things up?" If so, then keep these two things in mind:
1. **If you do this as a team, getting estimates from the people who will be doing the work,** you are likely to make more accurate estimates.
2. **Your guesses are probably more accurate and realistic than you think!** Remember, you have likely had many solid experiences that will help you intuitively make good judgments. (See the 2nd half of this eBook, The People Stuff: 10 Sets of Challenges to Inspire Teams… **"Trust Your Judgment."**)

Step 6: Build a schedule.

Overview
There are two main reasons for creating a project schedule:
- To help coordinate the work of project team members by keeping them focused on upcoming tasks, deadlines, elapsed project time, and remaining project time.
- To help communicate with people outside the project about project goals, deadlines, status, and so on. (In fact, sometimes a beautifully prepared schedule can help "sell" the project and help convince senior managers or customers that their support will be going to a well-conceived project.)

In the preceding steps we identified project tasks and figured out how long each should take. So now it's possible to tie these tasks and timeframes to actual calendar dates and create one or more project schedules. These may then be displayed as Gantt charts, network diagrams, milestone charts, or text tables. (See Sample Project Schedules below.)

Results
- One or more overview schedules showing the "big picture" of the project (i.e., showing all activities, phases, and major milestones*). Overview schedules can take any graphical or text form, depending on the preferences of the team and the ability of the particular schedule type to clearly show project events.
- One or more detailed schedules that expand or "zoom in" on particular parts of the overview schedule. Such detailed schedules might show:
  - One particular project phase and all the detailed subtasks and tasks that occur in that phase.
  - The tasks of particular project players. (For example, you might have a unique schedule showing only the plumbers' tasks or a schedule showing only the computer programmers' tasks, or a schedule showing only the senior executives' review & approval points.)
- A strategy to revisit the schedule periodically in order to keep it up to date.

Process

1. Assemble all project documentation completed in the earlier steps, including the approved Project Scope Statement, WBS, network diagram, task lists, estimates of effort/duration, technical specifications, proposals, and so on.
2. Assemble the core project team. (You don't need all the stakeholders for this step. The core team – people who will be directly creating the project deliverables* – can determine the project schedule.)
3. Conduct a brainstorming session in which the core project team creates a list of the particular types of schedules they would find most useful. In particular, decide on the format (Gantt chart, network diagram, etc.) and how frequently they should be updated.
4. Create one or more project schedules.
5. Circulate the schedules to all project stakeholders and provide explanations of symbols or special terms used, deadlines or bottle necks shown, and anything else you need to highlight to help coordinate your project team.
6. Get approval of your schedules from key stakeholders and the project sponsor.

The Minimalist Squeeze

Use the Minimalist approach to create and refine your schedule.

1. Create the schedule with the easiest-to-use software available. You don't need to use project management software. (See the *Note* below.)
2. Review your schedule and analyze the flow of tasks and activities. Ask:
   - Are there opportunities to streamline our work process?
   - Should we refine (preferably reduce) our estimates of time, effort and resources?
   - Is the schedule as clean and as "tight" as it might be?
3. Use these Minimalist Values to guide you here:
   - Work as fast as quality permits – maybe faster!
   - Deliver something – anything – as soon as possible.
   - Ignore external-to-the-project "professionals" who would have you puff up the project or its work processes.
   - Do less work.

Note: You do NOT need to use project management software to create the project schedule, though such products can certainly be useful. You can create perfectly fine Gantt charts and other forms of schedules using the tables or graphics feature in your word processor or spreadsheet program. You can apply your imagination to create multi-color cells for tasks, add connector lines, and so on. Both these kinds of programs (for example, MS Word or Excel) allow you to do clean and simple graphical annotations and then… voila! … You have a perfectly useful schedule. On the other hand, If you'd like to explore different types of PM software packages, go to the links page *"PM Software"* at **Michael Greer's Project Management Resources**
(http://michaelgreer.biz/?page_id=241) and look for free trials of PM software available for download.

Sample Project Schedules:

Below are some sample project schedules. Examine each of them and ask yourself:
- What are the strengths and weaknesses of this type of schedule?
- Which type would best show the structure of my project – the way work flows and is handed off from person to person.
- Which of these schedule types should I use to communicate with my stakeholders and core team to better coordinate my project?

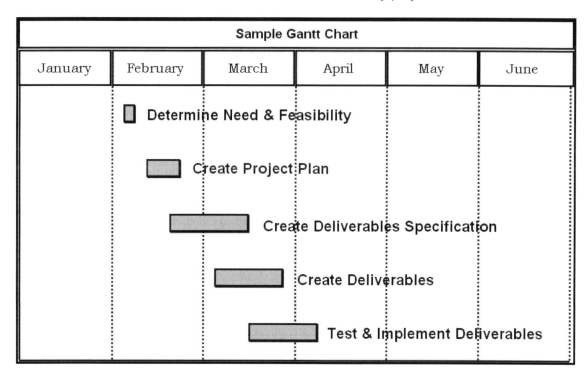

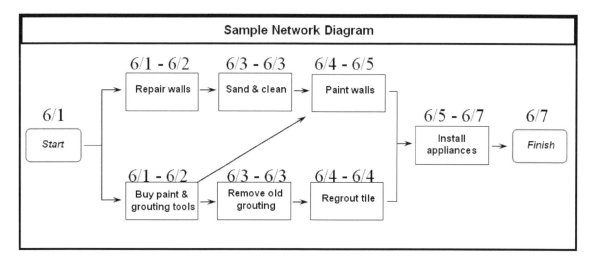

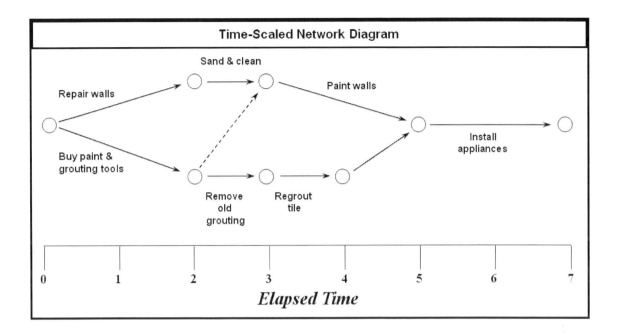

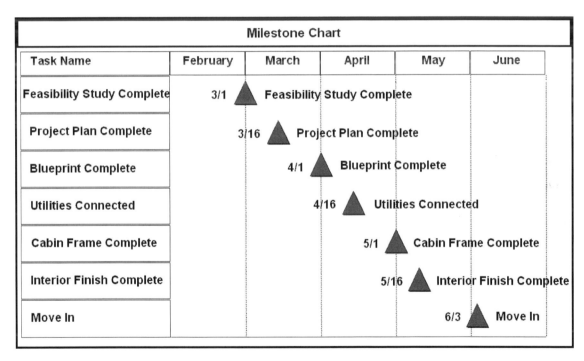

Ordinary Calendar						
Sun	Mon	Tue	Wed	Thur	Fri	Sat
1 * Repair * Buy Paint, Tools	2 Walls	3 * Sand, Etc..	4 * Paint walls * Regrout tile	5	6 * Install Appliances	7
8	9 * Shop around for new game room components	10	11	12	13	14 →
15	16	17	18	19 →	20 * Design new game room	21
22	23	24	25	26	27	28
29	30	31				

Sample Text Table	
Date	*Activity*
Jan. 15–Mar. 15	Conduct research
Mar. 16–Apr. 16	Create detailed deliverables specifications
Apr. 16–Apr. 26	Sponsor review of detailed deliverables specifications

[Samples are from The Project Manager's Partner, 2nd Edition, © Copyright 2001, Michael Greer/HRD Press]

Step 7: Estimate the costs.

Overview

Cost estimates are your best guess of the costs of the resources you will need to complete the project tasks. Cost estimates should cover labor, materials, supplies, and miscellaneous items such as inflation, administrative costs, and so on. Cost estimates are frequently refined (adjusted) throughout the project to reflect the project team's better understanding of the actual deliverables as they evolve.

In Step 5 you created your estimate of time, effort, and resources needed. Now it's time to translate this into a cost estimate.

Note: In many organizations, project managers manage their projects without any estimates of project costs. That's okay! If you have created a schedule and an estimate of effort and resources, these may be used as references to help keep the project on track. By making sure that the effort actually expended by workers is within the amount of effort estimated, you will be indirectly managing the main costs of most projects: the cost of labor.

Results

- An estimate of project costs, including the costs of labor, materials, supplies, and any other costs that are tracked by your organization, such as various overhead costs, profit, and so on.
- A description of all assumptions made in the cost estimate (i.e., "We are assuming an hourly rate of $75/hour for a particular type of worker or a per unit rental fee of $2000/month for a particular piece of equipment.)

Process:

1. Assemble all project documentation completed in the earlier steps, including the approved Project Scope Statement, WBS, network diagram, task lists, estimates of effort/duration, technical specifications, proposals, and so on.
2. Assemble the core project team. (You don't need all the stakeholders for this step. The core team – the people who will be completing the project tasks – can determine the project costs.)
3. Conduct a cost estimating session in which the core project team reviews the Effort/Duration table created in Step 5, and then creates a project cost estimate. (See Sample Cost Estimation Worksheet below.)
4. Circulate the Cost Estimate to all project stakeholders and provide explanations of any assumptions.
5. Get approval of your Cost Estimate from key stakeholders and the project sponsor.

The Minimalist Squeeze

Use the Minimalist approach to refine your cost estimate.
1. Challenge the idea that you need a cost estimate. (See discussion above.) If most of your costs are labor costs, then you can control costs indirectly by simply

making sure you labor hours don't go over those estimated. So why bother creating a cost estimate?
2. If you must create a cost estimate, do so with the easiest-to-use software. A simple Word or Excel table will probably do just fine.
3. Review your cost estimate and analyze the large dollar items. Ask:
    - Are there costs we could eliminate by simply buying what we need, pre-made, instead of investing labor dollars in making it ourselves?
    - Could we save money by using outside contractors to do some of the work or student interns or less-skilled people?
    - Are there things we are buying or suppliers we are buying from that we should challenge? (Are we simply buying out of habit or out of policy, instead of buying because we are getting something we really need at the best possible price?)
    - Can people use less-costly supplies, equipment, or tools?
    - Might we use online resources to replace the cost of buying expensive individual software or to host online meetings/reviews instead of spending money and time on travel?
4. Use these Minimalist Values to guide you here:
    - Ignore external-to-the-project "professionals" who would have you puff up the project or its work processes.
    - Create fewer deliverables with fewer features.
    - Do less work.

Sample Cost Estimation Worksheet

As you can see from the sample below, it's a fairly straightforward process to create a project cost estimate – once you have created the Effort/Duration table and other project planning artifacts in the previous Steps.

Sample Cost Estimation Worksheet

Activity	Duration	Resource Name: Laborer Resource Rate: $10 / hour Cost of Resource for This Activity	Resource Name: Truck Driver/ Laborer Resource Rate: $15 / hour Cost of Resource for This Activity	Resource Name: Supervisor/ Laborer Resource Rate: $20 / hour Cost of Resource for This Activity	Misc. Costs	Total Costs, Activity
Travel to site	1 hr.	$10.00	$15.00	$20.00	$150.00 (Rent truck)	$195.00
Determine strategy for clean up	.5 hr.	$5.00	$7.50	$10.00		$22.50
Remove brush	3 hr.	$30.00	$45.00	$60.00		$135.00
Load brush in truck	1 hr.	$10.00	$15.00	$20.00		$45.00
Haul brush to landfill	.5 hr.	$5.00	$7.50	$10.00		$22.50
Unload brush at landfill	1 hr.	$10.00	$15.00	$20.00	$25.00 (Dump fee)	$70.00
Return from site	1 hr.	$10.00	$15.00	$20.00		$45.00
Return truck	.5 hr.			$10.00		$10.00
Total:	8.5	$80.00	$120.00	$170.00	$175.00	$545.00

[Sample is from The Project Manager's Partner, 2nd Edition, © Copyright 2001, Michael Greer/HRD Press]

Note: This example is overly simplified in order to illustrate the relationship among cost elements. However, when you plan your projects, you will likely need to add many more columns for resources and break down "Misc. Costs" into subcategories based on the deliverables you are creating. In addition, you should consider adding blanks for contingency fees, administrative costs, profit, and other items related to your particular organization's needs.

Step 8: Keep the project moving.

Overview

If you've completed the previous seven Steps, you have assembled quite a collection of documents that can help you manage the project! In summary, you have built yourself the following:
- Project Charter
- Description of project roles, responsibilities, authority
- Description of specific deliverables (WBS) and Project Scope Statement
- Project task list, organized into phases and/or a network diagram
- Effort/Duration table
- One or more schedules
- Cost estimate

Each of these documents listed above (or project artifacts, as I like to call them) provides you with a yardstick for measuring some aspect of the project. And because each of them has been formally approved by stakeholders and the project sponsor, they may be considered an "official" set of guidelines for everybody on the project team to follow.

If you are a vendor providing the project deliverables for a client, these documents constitute your contract with your client. If you are a project manager working inside an organization, these documents constitute the commitments made by you and all other project stakeholders to perform an exact set of tasks and create an exact set of deliverables. On the other hand, **any deliverables or tasks that are not specified in these documents should not be undertaken by the project team because they are not part of the overall, agreed-upon project plan.** In other words, these documents summarize the shared vision and promises you and all stakeholders made to each other.

The bottom line is this: This collection of documents is the most important set of tools the project manager has for keeping the project moving toward completion. **By comparing the actual progress of your project to the promises made in these documents, you can make sure that your project is proceeding as planned.**

Results

This Step, Keep the Project Moving, should result in:
- Periodic progress checks of each dimension of the project as spelled out in the project artifacts listed above (Charter, Effort/Duration table, Schedule, Cost Estimate, etc.)
- Project manager inspection and awareness of overall progress toward completion
- Project manager interventions to correct problems, remove obstacles, and keep the project moving as planned

Process

After your project is up and running, you can use the checklist below and the artifacts you created in Steps 1 – 7 to help you keep things moving. Revisit these weekly.

Checklist: Keep the Project Moving

Go through this list at least weekly for each project you are managing.

❑ **CHECK YOUR PROJECT'S SCOPE.**

Refresh your memory about your project's goals and boundaries. In particular, make sure you have a clear picture of what the desired results should be at this point relative to deliverables, schedule, costs, quality, and so on.

(Refer to your Project Charter, specific deliverables (WBS) and Project Scope Statement)

❑ **CHECK YOUR DELIVERABLES (WORK PRODUCTS).**

Analyze the status of each deliverable. Are they evolving as planned? If appropriate:

1. Locate *any quality criteria* that may be applied to inspect the quality and completeness of the deliverables at this *stage* of the project.
2. Check *contractors' proposals or contracts* to make sure you know what they should be supplying at this point.
3. Inspect all project deliverables.
4. Decide whether to accept inspected deliverables or to require rework.

(Refer to your Project Charter, specific deliverables (WBS) and Project Scope Statement)

❑ **CHECK YOUR SCHEDULE.**

Examine your milestones, key dates, and phases. Are you where you need to be?

❑ **ANALYZE VARIANCES (DEVIATIONS FROM PLAN) BY COMPARING "ESTIMATED" TO "ACTUAL."**

1. Are activities taking longer than planned? (Are you exceeding estimates of duration?)
2. Are you using more resource hours than you planned?
3. Are your actual costs exceeding your estimated costs?
4. If minor variances are discovered (variances that can be resolved easily without changing the plan or scope), then resolve them.
5. If major variances are discovered (variances that change the scope or constitute significant project issues), then handle them as described in the steps below.

(Refer to your WBS, Schedule, Effort/Duration table, Cost Estimate.)

Continued on Next Page….

Checklist: Keep the Project Moving (cont'd)

- **ADDRESS SCOPE CHANGES.**
    1. Identify changes in scope (changes in deliverables, schedule, costs, etc.).
    2. Handle scope changes, if necessary.

    (See Step 9, Handle Scope Changes and Worksheet: Project Scope Change Order, below.)

- **LIST, TRACK, AND TRY TO RESOLVE OPEN ISSUES.**
    1. Make a list of all the unresolved issues, or
    2. Revisit the list of open issues from the last inspection period and try to resolve them.

- **REVISIT POTENTIAL PROJECT RISKS.**
    1. Locate any informal list of project risks that you are tracking or the formal Risk Management Plan, if one has been created.
    2. Note particularly whether any of the ongoing events or upcoming events are identified in the risk management plan as particularly vulnerable to risk.

- **REPORT PROJECT STATUS AND COMMUNICATE REGULARLY.**
    1. After completing the checks above, if you haven't already done so, talk to your team members and determine their perspectives on project status.
    2. Create and circulate a project status report.
    3. Create and distribute other project updates and communications as needed.

    (See Worksheets: The Project Status Report, & Project Communications Planner, below.)

- **DRIVE FOR CLOSE-OUT OF ACTIVITIES AND SIGN-OFF OF DELIVERABLES AS APPROPRIATE.**
    1. Keep asking yourself, "What activities can I close out? Which deliverables can I get formally approved and signed-off?"
    2. Prepare and get signatures on sign-off forms as appropriate.

    (See Worksheet: Sample Project Sign-off Form under Step 10: Close Out…below.)

- **CREATE A LIST OF LESSONS LEARNED.**

    Create a list of lessons learned that describes the ways subsequent project activities must be modified in order to prevent the difficulties encountered up to this point.

- **COMPLETE APPROPRIATE EVALUATION CHECKLISTS.**

    Complete evaluation checklists, if applicable, and file them as part of the official project records.

[Adapted from The Project Manager's Partner, 2nd Edition, © Copyright 2001, Michael Greer/HRD Press]

The Minimalist Squeeze

Use the Minimalist approach to help you keep the project moving.

1. Challenge the idea that you need meetings of any kind. Instead:
   - Replace meetings with "management by walking around" (MBWA). This way you can informally check progress without disrupting peoples' work.
   - Replace status meetings with "rolled up" status reports. Have each team member work from a task list which they simply update weekly. Then you can compile these updates into a summary status report. This can be emailed and discussed via phone call, if necessary.
   - If a team member has questions about a design or an approach, go to his work space and discuss the thing itself, live and in person, on the spot. This can be faster than forcing him to organize a presentation and then have everyone talking about it in generalities in a meeting.
2. If you must have a meeting, make sure you have a good reason for inviting each person who is attending. If you're not sure they are needed in the meeting, ask them to simply give you a note or list of questions that you can present on their behalf. Then spare them from the meeting and keep them working.
3. Protect your task specialists from administrivia. If there are reports to be filed or "dog and pony show" appearances to be made, get the details from them and then create the report or make the appearance yourself. Let them keep working.
4. Use these Minimalist Values to guide you here:
   - Ignore external-to-the-project "professionals" who would have you puff up the project or its work processes.
   - "Make it real" as often as possible with models, mock-ups, prototypes, & samples. (This helps avoid rework and wasting time in abstract arguments.)
   - Work as fast as quality permits – maybe faster!
   - Do less work.

Worksheet: The Project Status Report

Title: [Project Name] Status Report
Date:
Author:

Accomplishments Since Last Report:
(Deliverables completed, milestones attained, decisions made, issues resolved, etc.)
-

-

-

Upcoming Activities:
(What the team must focus on accomplishing throughout the next reporting period.)
-

-

Summary of Issues, Concerns, and Recommended Actions:
(What issues or concerns are unresolved? Include recommended actions for each.)
-

-

Comments:
(Miscellaneous comments, public praise for extra effort, announcements, etc.)
-

-

[This tool is from The Project Manager's Partner, 2nd Edition, © Copyright 2001, Michael Greer/HRD Press]

The Project Management Minimalist: Just Enough PM to Rock Your Projects!

Worksheet: Project Communications Planner

Instructions: Using the chart below...

- ❑ In the **Who (Receiver)** column, list all the different project stakeholders who will be needing information as the project unfolds. (You may want to list some stakeholders as a group, such as "IT" or "Finance." However, be careful that you have a clear idea about the specific people within the group to whom communications should be going.)

- ❑ In the **What Information** column, list the type of information this person or group will need.

- ❑ In the **When (How Often)** column, list how often or at what points in the project this person or group will need the information. (For example, you might say "weekly" or "monthly" here, or "at sign-off of Phase II.")

- ❑ In the **How (Form/Medium)** column, list the appropriate medium of communication. (For example, you might say "e-mail status report," "team meeting," "broadcast voice-mail," or "update to project web page.")

- ❑ In the **Who Creates & Publishes** column, list who will create and publish (i.e., distribute) the particular communication.

Who (Receiver)	*What Information*	*When (How Often)*	*How (Form/Medium)*	*Who Creates & Publishes*

Step 9: Handle scope changes.

Overview

Scope change may be defined as any addition, reduction, or modification to the deliverables or work process as outlined in your original project plan. Change of scope is normal — it's not necessarily a problem. In fact, scope changes can be beneficial when they allow the project team to respond sensibly to changing conditions that exist outside the project. This can help ensure that project deliverables remain relevant.

Project managers should approach changes of scope in a business-like (as opposed to emotional) fashion. The process below outlines a systematic process for dealing with scope change.

Results

- Adjustments to the project plan to deal with additions, reductions or modification to the deliverables or work process
- Formal documentation of each scope change
- Formal approval of each scope change

Process

Follow these steps to handle changes in scope:

1. **Stay calm.** Remind yourself that the original project scope documents were created at a time when you knew less than you know now. Given the new knowledge and circumstances, you need to modify your plan. This will likely result in your having to ask for more time, more resources, more money, and other concessions from your sponsors or stakeholders. Realize that you'll simply need to analyze the situation and make a solid case for your new requirements. So there's no need to panic.

2. **Pinpoint the exact change.** Clearly and dispassionately state the exact scope of the change that is required.

3. **Analyze the impact** of the change. Specify how the change will impact:
   - Schedule
   - Quality of the finished product
   - Costs
   - Project team assignments, including level of effort
   - Other deliverables, including their amount and quality

4. **Discuss the impact with your project team.** Assemble relevant team members and brainstorm alternatives for handling the change with as little impact as possible.

5. **Report the impact to the sponsor.** Make sure the sponsor is aware of implications of the change by discussing the change with the sponsor and his key

stakeholder-recommenders.

6. **Update the project scope statement and overall plan.** Make an addendum or a complete revision, if appropriate, of the project schedule, work breakdown structure, scope description, and so on. Make sure you note all of the conditions that led to the change, the people who discussed alternatives, and the people who selected the recommended alternative. Document it—**get it in writing.**

7. **Obtain written sponsor approval of the change and the corresponding revised plan.** To guard against "amnesia" on the part of the sponsor, make sure the sponsor signs a document acknowledging the scope change and its rationale.

The Minimalist Squeeze

Use the Minimalist approach to handle scope changes.

1. Isolate the scope change, if possible, and prevent it from having an impact on other project elements.
   - For example, if the change only impacts the work products of one team member, then don't bother involving everyone else in dealing with it.
2. Consider dropping the project component that is the subject of the scope change. Simply let it go and use the remaining deliverables without it.
3. Decide to temporarily live without the project component in question, then build it in the next project.
4. Use these Minimalist Values to guide you here:
   - Create fewer deliverables with fewer features.
   - Do less work.
   - Absorb or neutralize (but don't ignore) anyone who can reject or rethink your deliverables.
   - Deliver something – anything – as soon as possible.
   - Give up on the project earlier; cut your losses.
   - Ignore external-to-the-project "professionals" who would have you puff up the project or its work processes.

Worksheet: Project Scope Change Order

Project Name: _____   **Date:** _____
Project Manager: _____
Project Tracking Number: _____   **Change No.:** _____

Summary of Change:

Rationale for Change:

Brief overview of the impact of this change on . . .
- Project schedule:

- Quality of deliverables:

- Costs:

- Stakeholders and/or core team members:

- Other deliverables, including amount and quality:

Change approved by (signatures):

Sponsor: _____   Date: _____

Project Manager: _____   Date: _____

Other: _____   Date: _____

[This tool is from The Project Manager's Partner, 2nd Edition, © Copyright 2001, Michael Greer/HRD Press]

Step 10: Close out phases, close out the project.

Overview

As noted earlier, **projects, by definition, are temporary endeavors**. They must eventually come to an end. **So they are necessarily limited in the time and effort that can be consumed, as well as the resources that can be used.** For this reason, one of the most important things **(possibly the single most important thing) that a project manager can do is to drive the project toward completion.** But how do you know when the project is completed?

Project completion, at minimum, depends on two key activities:
- Formal **close out of phases** (as indicated by written approval, or sign-off, of the sponsor and/or official hand-off of deliverables as they are evolving in increments)
- Formal **close out of the entire project** (as indicated by written approval, or sign-off, of the sponsor and/or official hand-off of finished deliverables)

In addition, depending on your project, **close out activities could involve several other important chores** such as:
- Closing out vendor contracts
- Creating a project archive containing all project documentation
- Conducting a project "post mortem" and determining lessons learned
- Formally handing off project deliverables to end users
- Conducting training sessions to teach end users how to get the most out of the deliverables your project team has created
- Writing performance evaluations or letters of thanks for team members to place in their personnel files (and to help assure they want to work with you again!)

Results

- Sponsor sign-off and approval of incrementally-evolving project deliverables and phases as they are completed
- Sponsor sign-off and approval of all finished project deliverables and the overall completed project
- Completion of any of the project-specific follow-up activities named above (Project Archive, Post Mortem, Lessons Learned, hand-off/training, performance evaluations, etc.)

Process

1. Review your Project Scope Statement, your WBS or list of deliverables, and any Scope Change Orders that were approved during the project and determine whether everything has been completed and approved. (If there are any items not completed, discuss with your stakeholders and sponsor how you will deal with these.)
2. Conduct any formal evaluations or acceptance tests and create reports of the results.

3. Close out vendor contracts and make sure all related paperwork (formal approval of work products, tax info, etc.) has been submitted.
4. Submit any internal paperwork indicating the close of the project.
5. Assemble all relevant project documentation into a Project Archive (binder or disk-based)
6. Hand off deliverables to the sponsor and/or end users, providing any training or special instructions for use.
7. Conduct a Project "Post Mortem" and create a list of Lessons Learned. (See Project "Post Mortem" Review Questions, below.)
8. Obtain formal approval, in the form of a written sign-off, for the entire project. (See Sample Project Sign-off Form, below.)
9. Find out from all stakeholders, particularly core team members, what kinds of documentation they would like to have created that formally recognizes their work on the project. (This might include formal performance review input for their personnel files, Thank You letters, etc.) Then create this documentation for each project team member.

The Minimalist Squeeze

Close out of phases and close out of the entire project is key to project management. And most of the results and processes listed above are essential. So it's tough to "squeeze out" any fluff in this Step. However, you might consider these suggestions to make sure your project is as lean as it can be during all close-out processes.

1. Look at the items in the list above (… the nine Processes). Ask:
   - Is each task relevant to my project? (Could I simply drop some?)
   - Might I replace face-to-face close-out meetings with video or audio conferences?
   - Can I use the archived documents from similar projects to serve as templates or models when archiving my project?
   - How can I reduce the number of people who must be involved in each process?
   - *CAUTION: Do **not** minimize or drop your requirement for formal, written approval – i.e., sign off – of project phases and at the end of the project. Verbal approval is not enough.*
2. Use these Minimalist Values to guide you:
   - Do less work.
   - Work as fast as quality permits – maybe faster!
   - Give up on the project earlier; cut your losses.
   - Ignore external-to-the-project "professionals" who would have you puff up the project or its work processes.

Worksheet: Sign-Off Form [For a Project Phase]

Project Name: XYZ System Upgrade

I have reviewed the following deliverables as of the date identified below:

-
-
-

I have found these deliverables to meet with my approval, with the following exceptions:

-
-
-

I hereby give my approval to proceed with the evolution of these deliverables to the next stage of development in order to meet the project objectives in a timely fashion.

I understand that any changes (additions, deletions, or modifications) to the fundamental structure, underlying design, or the specific features of these deliverables might result in:

- Slippage of the completion date for these deliverables

- Additional resource requirements

- Additional costs

_____ **[Signature]**
John Doe, V.P.
Corporate Cosmic Vision

Date:_____

[This tool is from The Project Manager's Partner, 2nd Edition, © Copyright 2001, Michael Greer/HRD Press]

Worksheet: Project Sign-Off Form [For an Entire Project]

Project Name: XYZ System Upgrade

I have reviewed the following finished deliverables as of the date identified below:

- *[insert names of specific deliverables to be approved here]*

-

-

I have found these finished deliverables to meet with my approval, with the following exceptions:

- *[insert names of specific deliverables that are not approved here]*

-

-

For each of the deliverables that are named above as exceptions, we will proceed as follows with the following remedies within the time frames specified:

- *[Describe remedies to be taken to correct the deliverables and deadlines for achieving the remedies.]*

-

-

-

_____ *[Signature]*
John Doe, V.P.
Corporate Cosmic Vision

Date:_____

Project "Post Mortem" Review Questions

It's important for project managers and team members to take stock at the end of a project and develop a list of lessons learned so that they don't repeat their mistakes in the next project. Typically such reviews are called post-project reviews or "post mortems."

We recommend **a two-step process for conducting these reviews:**
- First, prepare and circulate a whole bunch of specific questions about the project and give team members time to think about them and prepare their responses individually.
- Next, hold a meeting and discuss the team's responses to the questions. The result of this discussion is often a list of "Lessons Learned."

The benefit of the first step, done individually by team members, is that it allows the quieter, more analytical people to develop their responses to the questions without being interrupted by the more outgoing, vocal people who might otherwise dominate in the face-to-face meeting. Also, it allows everyone the time to create more thoughtful responses.

So what would be on the list of questions? We've provided some of our favorites below.

General Questions

1. Are you proud of our finished deliverables (project work products)? If yes, what's so good about them? If no, what's wrong with them?
2. What was the single most frustrating part of our project?
3. How would you do things differently next time to avoid this frustration?
4. What was the most gratifying or professionally satisfying part of the project?
5. Which of our methods or processes worked particularly well?
6. Which of our methods or processes were difficult or frustrating to use?
7. If you could wave a magic wand and change anything about the project, what would you change?
8. Did our stakeholders, senior managers, customers, and sponsor(s) participate effectively? If not, how could we improve their participation?

Phase-Specific Questions *(These will differ from project to project, depending on the project's life cycle/phases. The phases identified below are fully explained in the discussion of our Generic Project Life Cycle from Part I of The Project Manager's Partner, 2nd Edition.)*

Phase I: Determine Need and Feasibility

1. Did our needs/market analysis or feasibility study identify all the project deliverables that we eventually had to build? If not, what did we miss and how can we be sure our future analyses don't miss such items?
2. Did our needs/market analysis or feasibility study identify unnecessary deliverables? If so, how can we be sure our future analyses don't make this mistake?
3. How could we have improved our need-feasibility or analysis phase?

Phase II: Create Project Plan

1. How accurate were our original estimates of the size and effort of our project? What did we over or under estimate? (Consider deliverables, work effort, materials required, etc.)
2. How could we have improved our estimate of size and effort so that it was more accurate?
3. Did we have the right people assigned to all project roles? (Consider subject matter expertise, technical contributions, management, review and approval, and other key roles) If no, how can we make sure that we get the right people next time?

4. Describe any early warning signs of problems that occurred later in the project? How should we have reacted to these signs? How can we be sure to notice these early warning signs next time?
5. Could we have completed this project without one or more of our vendors/contractors? If so, how?
6. Were our constraints, limitations, and requirements made clear to all vendors/contractors from the beginning? If not, how could we have improved our RFP or statement of need?
7. Were there any difficulties negotiating the vendor contract? How could these have been avoided?
8. Were there any difficulties setting up vendor paperwork (purchase orders, contracts, etc.) or getting the vendor started? How could these have been avoided?
9. List team members or stakeholders who were missing from the kickoff meeting or who were not involved early enough in our project. How can we avoid these oversights in the future?
10. Were all team/stakeholder roles and responsibilities clearly delineated and communicated? If not, how could we have improved these?
11. Were the deliverables specifications, milestones, and specific schedule elements/dates clearly communicated? If not, how could we improve this?

Phase III: Create Specifications for Deliverables

1. Were you proud of our blueprints or other detailed design specifications? If not, how could we have improved these?
2. Did all the important project players have creative input into the creation of the design specifications? If not, who were we missing and how can we assure their involvement next time?
3. Did those who reviewed the design specifications provide timely and meaningful input? If not, how could we have improved their involvement and the quality of their contributions?
4. How could we have improved our work process for creating deliverables specifications?
[Insert your own, deliverables-specific questions here.]

Phase IV: Create Deliverables

1. Were you proud of our deliverables? If not, how could we have improved these?
2. Did all the important project players have creative input into the creation of the deliverables? If not, who were we missing and how can we assure their involvement next time?
3. Did those who reviewed the deliverables provide timely and meaningful input? If not, how could we have improved their involvement and the quality of their contributions?
4. How could we have improved our work process for creating deliverables?
[Insert your own, deliverables-specific questions here.]

Phase V: Test and Implement Deliverables

1. Were the members of our test audience truly representative of our target audience? If not, how could we assure better representation in the future?
2. Did the test facilities, equipment, materials, and support people help to make the test an accurate representation of how the deliverables will be used in the "real world?" If not, how could we have improved on these items?
3. Did we get timely, high-quality feedback about how we might improve our deliverables? If not, how could we get better feedabck in the future?
4. Was our implementation strategy accurate and effective? How could we improve this strategy?
5. Did our hand-off of deliverables to the user/customer/sponsor represent a smooth and easy transition? If not, how could we have improved this process?
[Insert your own, deliverables-specific questions here.]

[This tool is from The Project Manager's Partner, 2nd Edition, © Copyright 2001, Michael Greer/HRD Press]

Conclusion

This part of the book, *The Nuts and Bolts: 10 Steps to Project Success* provided you with "just enough" information and tools to help perform these key PM steps:

- Step 1: Define the project concept, then get support and approval.
- Step 2: Get your team together and start the project.
- Step 3: Figure out exactly what the finished work product will be.
- Step 4: Figure out what you need to do to complete the work products. (Identify tasks and phases.)
- Step 5: Estimate time, effort, and resources.
- Step 6: Build a schedule.
- Step 7: Estimate the costs.
- Step 8: Keep the project moving.
- Step 9: Handle scope changes.
- Step 10: Close out phases, close out the project.

As I said in the *Introduction* (and as you can see from the preceding tools and guidelines) **project management (PM) is not rocket science!** The basic PM tools and processes presented in these 10 Steps are straightforward and fairly easy to use. So I hope you put some of them to work on your next project. They'll help you create a project that is well-organized and completed on time, on budget, and with excellent results.

Summary & Checklist: 10 Steps to Project Success

Step	Results of Successful Performance
1. Define the project concept, then get support and approval.	❏ A series of conversations, brainstorming sessions, and other formal or informal discussions about the project concept with your supervisor and key people whom you hope will provide project support ❏ An approved **Project Charter**
2. Get your team together and start the project.	❏ A series of conversations, brainstorming sessions, and other formal/informal discussions about the project concept with all stakeholders ❏ *Commitments from stakeholders* to play particular roles on the project team throughout or at specific times in the project. ❏ *Written documentation* that captures roles and responsibilities of all stakeholders ❏ A **Kickoff Meeting** that orients all project team members to their roles and responsibilities and gets the project started (often supported by a **Responsibility/Accountability Matrix**)
3. Figure out exactly what the finished work products will be.	❏ A series of conversations, brainstorming sessions, and other formal/informal discussions about specific project deliverables ❏ A **Work Breakdown Structure (WBS)** in rough form as created by a brainstorming group (i.e., a bunch of yellow stickies spread out all over a wall, a collection of flip chart pages scribbled with items, a rough "mind map," etc.) ❏ A polished WBS which clearly lists 1) all interim deliverables that the end user will not see (such as scripts, flow charts, outlines, etc.) and 2) all finished deliverables that will be turned over to the user when the project is completed. ❏ A **Project Scope Statement** that expands the Project Charter to include the WBS and other items identified by the team in brainstorming sessions ❏ **Approval of the Project Scope Statement and WBS** by the sponsor and appropriate stakeholders.
4. Figure out what you need to do to complete the work products. (Identify tasks and phases.)	❏ A list or graphical collection of *all project tasks* that must be completed to create project deliverables. ❏ A *network diagram* showing the *sequence and flow* of all project tasks, including opportunities for stakeholders to review and approve deliverables as they evolve ❏ Descriptions or illustrations of project phases
5. Estimate time, effort, and resources.	❏ A detailed estimate of the *duration, effort, and resources required* to complete each project task ❏ A summary of duration, effort, and resources required for the entire project
6. Build a schedule.	❏ One or more *overview schedules* showing the "big picture" of the project (i.e., showing all activities, phases, and major milestones). (Gantt, network diagram, summary table/calendar, etc.) ❏ One or more *detailed schedules* that expand or "zoom in" on particular parts of the overview schedule. (E.g., One particular project phase w/ detailed subtasks/tasks or one particular set of project players. (i.e., plumbers, computer programmers, senior executives w/approval points.) ❏ A *strategy to revisit* the schedule periodically in order to keep it up to date.
7. Estimate the costs.	❏ An *estimate of project costs*, including the costs of labor, materials, supplies, and any other costs tracked by your organization, such as various overhead costs, etc. ❏ A description of all *assumptions made* in the cost estimate
8. Keep the project moving.	❏ Periodic *progress checks* of each dimension of the project as spelled out in the project artifacts above (Charter, Effort/Duration table, Schedule, Cost Estimate, etc.) ❏ *Project manager inspection* and awareness of overall progress toward completion ❏ *Project manager interventions* to correct problems, remove obstacles, and keep the project moving
9. Handle scope changes.	❏ *Adjustments to the project plan to deal with additions, reductions or modifications* to the deliverables or work process ❏ *Formal documentation* of each scope change ❏ *Formal approval* of each scope change
10. Close out phases, close out the project.	❏ Sponsor *sign-off/approval of incrementally-evolving project deliverables & phases* as completed ❏ Sponsor *sign-off/approval of all finished project deliverables* and the overall completed project ❏ *Completion of typical project-specific follow-up activities* (Project Archive, Post Mortem, Lessons Learned, hand-off/training, performance evaluations, etc.)

Additional Resources

Here are some **additional no-nonsense resources** related to PM that you might find valuable. They are available at my website, http://michaelgreer.biz

Plain and Simple PM Advice

- **Ten Guaranteed Ways to Screw Up Any Project** - http://michaelgreer.biz/?p=121
- **14 Key Principles for Project Success** -- http://michaelgreer.biz/?p=125
- **The Accidental Project Manager** -- http://michaelgreer.biz/?p=131
- **Too Many Projects? Prioritize Them!** -- http://michaelgreer.biz/?p=138
- **What's Project Portfolio Management (PPM) and Why Should Project Managers Care About It?** -- http://michaelgreer.biz/?p=147

Going a Bit Deeper into PM

- **The Project Manager's Partner, 2nd Edition** (My textbook. This is the source of most of the content in the preceding Steps!) -- http://michaelgreer.biz/?p=208
- **Summary of Key Project Manager Actions and Results** -- http://michaelgreer.biz/?p=118
- **Project Life Cycles versus Key PM Processes** -- http://michaelgreer.biz/?p=430
- **The New Project Manager's Support Pyramid: A Framework for PM Training & Support** -- http://michaelgreer.biz/?p=205

More Good Stuff on PM

- **My PM Links at Michael Greer's Project Management Resources** -- http://michaelgreer.biz/?page_id=233
- **My Customized, On-Site Custom Workshops** – http://michaelgreer.biz/?page_id=55
- **My Blog Posts** -- http://michaelgreer.biz/?page_id=364

How to Contact or Follow Me

- **My Website**, Michael Greer's Project Management Resources: http://michaelgreer.biz (blog posts: http://michaelgreer.biz/?page_id=364)
- **My Blog, Inspired Project Teams:** http://www.inspiredprojectteams.com/
- **Email:** pm.minimalist@gmail.com
- **Phone (24-hour voicemail): (530) 688-6613**
- **LinkedIn Profile:** http://www.linkedin.com/in/greerspmresources
- **Twitter feed:** http://twitter.com/michael_greerhttp://twitter.com/michael_greer
- **Facebook Profile:** http://profile.to/michael_greer

The People Stuff: 10 Sets of Challenges to Inspire Teams

This part of the book will help you inspire and motivate your project team. It might also help you reduce some of the contentious, unpleasant, or inappropriate stuff that sometimes plagues project teams. And yes, the topics are a bit philosophical. But each item also includes specific **performance-based Challenges** that you can immediately put to work with your project team. In all, there are 10 sets of Challenges selected from my *Inspired Project Teams blog.*

Each set of Challenges includes:

- **Quotations, war stories, examples, and a little philosophy** that can inspire project managers and project team members.
- **Reflections** for you to think about… as project manager or project leader.
- **Team Challenges** – Questions and suggestions to challenge your teams to stretch and grow.
- **Project Manager Challenges** – Specific actions you can take as project manager or team leader.
- **Learn More**… – Books and audio references (with links) that can help you learn more about the topic of each particular set of Challenges.

May these help your project team go from this … to this!

The 10 Sets of Challenges

Here's an overview of the 10 sets of Challenges presented in this part of the book:

- **Trust Your Judgment** – Many wise teachers and philosophers say that to achieve anything great you must trust that voice which lies deep within you. This post/podcast examines why this voice is trustworthy and how you can trust it.

- **Let Go of Perfectionism** – Are you driven to perfection? … or simply driven crazy? This post/podcast provides suggestions for project managers and team leaders about how they can let go of perfectionism and improve their results.

- **Celebrate the Chaos Within** – "One must still have chaos in oneself to be able to give birth to a dancing star." – Friedrich Nietzsche. This post/podcast provides suggestions on how project managers & leaders can support creativity.

- **Embrace the Work Itself** – So where's the joy in the work itself? What about the intrinsic value of our chosen profession? The beauty and fascination of the field itself?

- **Take the Risk** – This post is all about getting outside your comfort zone…If you can imagine it… if you can see it clearly… if it gets you excited as a possibility, then it may be your destiny to make it a reality.

- **Just Say No** – While it might make sense for individuals to say "yes" to life as often as they can, there are critical moments when project teams have just gotta say "no!" Here's why & how…

- **Listen, Understand, Collaborate** – "Habit 5: Seek First to Understand, Then to be Understood." – Stephen Covey's Seven Habits of Highly Effective People – This examines why & how project teams should listen, understand, & collaborate.

- **Just Do It!** – Get moving… get unstuck… & just do it! If you and your project team members are sometimes plagued with fits of analysis paralysis or procrastination, then this set of Challenges is for you.

- **Consciously Choose Your Attitude** – A project team's attitude can make or break the project. In this post learn how you can consciously choose your attitude instead of simply allowing it to overtake you as a collection of random feelings.

- **Be the Change You Want to See** -- "You must be the change you want to see in the world." - Mahatma Gandhi

HEY, LISTEN!
These and many more Challenges not included here are **available as FREE audio downloads (MP3 files)** from my blog **Inspired Project Teams blog**:
http://www.inspiredprojectteams.com/)
or from iTunes:
(http://itunes.apple.com/WebObjects/MZStore.woa/wa/viewPodcast?id=307055288)

Trust Your Judgment

"A man should learn to detect and watch that gleam of light which flashes across his mind from within, more than the luster of the firmament of bards and sages... Trust thyself: every heart vibrates to that iron string." **Ralph Waldo Emerson** in *Self-Reliance*

"... the best in every business do what they have learned to do without questioning their abilities — they flat out trust their skills, which is why we call this high-performance state of mind the 'Trusting Mindset.' Routine access to the Trusting Mindset is what separates great performers from the rest of the pack." -- **John Eliot** in *Overachievement*

"Skill in any performance, whether it be in sports, in playing the piano, in conversation, or in selling merchandise, consists not in painfully and consciously thinking out each action as it is performed, but in relaxing, and letting the job do itself through you. Creative performance is spontaneous and 'natural' as opposed to self-conscious and studied." **Maxwell Maltz** in *Psycho-Cybernetics*

"By banishing doubt and trusting your intuitive feelings, you clear a space for the power of intention to flow through." **Wayne Dyer** in *The Power of Intention*

So, do you trust yourself -- really trust yourself -- to come up with that creative leap, that exactly appropriate solution, that powerful insight that maybe no one else can generate?

The message shared by all these great teachers... indeed, by many other great philosophers... is that to achieve anything great you must trust that voice which lies deep within you and is trying to be heard. OK. If I could see you right now, I'm guessing some of you who are reading this are rolling your eyes and judging this all as a bit fluffy, cosmic, new agey, or "woo woo!" Still, I'm willing to bet that you (or some people you respect) have used one of these expressions:
- "I just had a hunch that..."
- "I had this strong intuition about..."
- "I had to go with my gut... I just did what seemed right."
- "I had a strong feeling about this and I just decided to follow my heart."

Whether you call it a "hunch," an "intuition," a "gut feeling," or simply the unspoken nudging of your heart, you're talking about pretty much the same thing: that inner voice of wisdom that we all possess, but we all too often stifle. Sure, this inner voice we're talking about can be intangible and elusive. But I bet that if you had to do so, you could logically trace the origins of its judgments and choices. And this logical audit trail would prove to you that this inner voice is really quite worthy of your trust and respect. Here's the deal: Your intuitions, "gut feelings," and hunches are derived from and ultimately grounded in your unique life experiences, both good and bad. And because of this, they have behind them the solid proof of your reality. To illustrate how all these experiences come together to generate solid, trustworthy judgments, I present to you the analogy of the common kitchen strainer. (Now stick with me, here... this is actually a pretty cool analogy!)

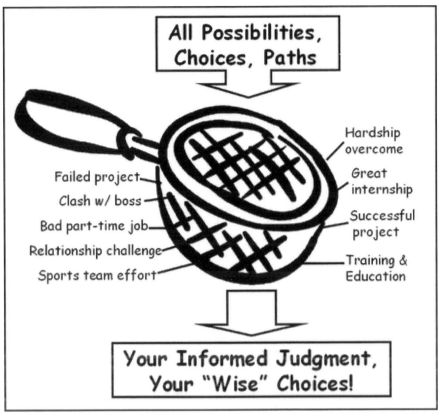

Your Inner Wisdom Filter: Why You Can Trust Your Judgment!

A kitchen strainer is made up of a whole bunch of strands of wire, criss-crossed to form a grid or a screen. Now let's say you don't have one of those fancy juice machines, but you want to mash up a bunch of fruit and extract the juice. You begin by cutting the fruit into pieces, then dump these pieces into the strainer. You then place the strainer over a bowl and push down on the fruit and mash it up until the juice runs into the bowl. The wire grid or screen of the strainer prevents all the seeds, stems, strands of bitter fibers, and fruit skins from coming through. The only thing you get in your bowl is the juice essence that you wanted. All that other stuff can be thrown out (or added to you favorite fiber-dense muffin dough!).

Your Inner Wisdom Filter

Your inner voice (i.e., your judgment) operates pretty much like that kitchen strainer! (*See graphic above.*) Let's say you have to make a difficult decision and don't have time to think about it. All sorts of possibilities and pertinent facts and constraints and outcomes rattle around in your brain. Your "internal strainer" is activated to deal with this. The wires in your internal strainer are made up of a vast set of unique experiences that you've acquired over your lifetime. Successes, failures, joys, miseries, and all sorts of life events combine to form this internal screening mechanism. That horrible job you had, that successful project, that challenge on your high school sports team, that class or internship you took, that difficult relationship you finally worked out -- all these events comprise the unique strainer that creates your special judgments. And when all the possible solutions and issues related to a problem are dumped into that strainer, the good stuff -- a unique and powerful judgment -- emerges. It's a judgment that's automatically informed by all of your life experiences. And, as such, it's powerful and trustworthy!

Still skeptical? Consider some real-life examples:

- **A badly battered and bleeding patient** is wheeled into the emergency room at a hospital. The on-call physician takes charge and begins diagnosing and treating the patient at a whirlwind pace. A life is at stake... there's no time to stop and think. Instead, the filter of the doctor's unique experiences (med school classes, internships, time served in the military, previous years working in an ER) -- this filter kicks in to quickly sort and choose among possible treatment strategies. Appropriate action is taken and a life is saved.

- **A wise tribal elder** is called on to mediate a dispute between neighbors. She doesn't need to consult legal texts or put the matter to a vote. She simply considers the situation in light of her years and years of life experiences and knowledge of the tribe, then makes her recommendation. The unique situation and options are filtered through her experiences and a trustworthy recommendation emerges.

- **Your grandpa** has been making his prize winning chili for many years. Somewhere back in his dim past, he used a recipe. But over time he's learned from making bad batches and good batches that a little more of this vegetable and a little of that spice added at just the right time in the cooking process results in chili that gets rave reviews. He'd be hard pressed to tell you exactly how he does it. The grid of his internal experiences simply produces high quality judgments automatically throughout the cooking process, while he's busy cutting up vegetables and stirring.

- Then there's **those fine artists we all admire.** They've been highly trained in brush selection and handling, paint mixing, composition, and so on. But when they start painting, they simply flow into the work. They allow the subject that inspires them to be strained through the grid of their training and unique sensibilities to create something that is beautiful and new. They trust their judgment.

- And finally, consider **the simple act of parallel parking** your car. As you align your tires to the curb and ease into the parking space, a thousand automatic muscle memories are activated to press the accelerator and the brake pedals at just the right times, turn the steering wheel just so, and scan your mirrors to get feedback on how you are doing. You don't tell your brain how to integrate all this hand-eye movement. Your internal filter simply takes in all the possibilities, sorts through them to figure out what really matters, and provides you with the judgment to park quickly and allow the other cars who are waiting for you to finish parking to be on their way.

The bottom line: You already HAVE trustworthy judgment! It's impossible to live your life without activating -- and trusting -- this judgment a thousand times a day! So why not really embrace it? Why not learn to trust your judgment whole-heartedly when you're making all those difficult professional decisions? Remember, deep down, you already know what you need to know!

Now let's apply all this to project management.

Challenges...

Reflections

Reflect on these questions:
- What are some of the complex things you do without thinking? (Consider sports, brain games, coaching, sifting & sorting through things, inspecting, quality assurance)
- If you had to do so, would you be able to dissect one of these complex abilities and show each skill and bit of knowledge and experience which makes you able to do this thing so well?
- When have you been under pressure to produce a fast decision on a complex issue? How did you fare? Was it a good decision? If you had to, could you defend it based on your experiences, skills, and training?
- What are some areas of your job or career where you might be overthinking things? Could you begin to relax and trust your judgment in these areas?

Team Challenges

Ask your team:
- Think about the projects you have worked on. When was the last time you had a really powerful experience of "I told you so!"
- Could this "I told you so..." event have been avoided if you had "spoken up," honoring that inner voice that knew better?
- Look back on your accumulated experiences and expertise. These are the sources of your judgment. How might we, as a project team, better leverage your judgment on our projects?
- What do you need from senior managers or project managers that would enable you to more confidently "trust yourself?"

Project Manager Challenges

- Take a few minutes to review each of your team members' resumes, job histories, and project track records. Look for signs of untapped wisdom.
- What parts of our projects are in need of some of the wisdom and judgment that our people may already have, but aren't using?
- Thinking about each team member and his or her experiences and expertise, ask yourself these questions:
  - Are we really using this person's judgment to the fullest extent?
  - Do we create a safe environment in which this person can apply their judgment?
  - Do I need to try to prove to this person that they can trust their judgment by pointing out their long history of successes and good decisions?
  - What can I do to help this person develop the confidence to more fully trust his or her judgment?

- What obstacles can I remove that are impeding them from exercising their judgment or are making them overly cautious?

Learn More...

- Go to **PhilosophersNotes** (http://www.philosophersnotes.com/) and download the full notes and MP3 versions of the following books:
  - *The Selected Writings of Ralph Waldo Emerson*
  - *Overachievement* by John Eliot
  - *Psycho-Cybernetics: A New Technique for Using Your Subconscious Power* by Maxwell Maltz
  - *The Power of Intention* by Dr. Wayne Dyer

- Get the *Essential Emerson CD*, narrated by Archibald Macleish, from LearnOutLoud.com. (http://www.learnoutloud.com/Product/E028499/81719)

- Get Wayne Dyer's 4 1/2 hr. abridged narration of *The Power of Intention* from LearnOutLoud.com. (http://www.learnoutloud.com/Product/3731/81719)

- For related **books** and **Kindle downloads** from **Amazon.com**, go to the *Inspired Project Teams blog post **"Trust Your Judgment"*** and **scroll to the end of the blog post.** Direct links to related Amazon products are posted there: http://www.inspiredprojectteams.com/?p=691

Let Go of Perfectionism

"The idea of perfect closes your mind to new standards.. When you drive hard toward one ideal, you miss opportunities and paths, not to mention hurting your confidence. Believe in your potential and then go out and explore it; don't limit it." **John Eliot, Ph.D**. in **Reverse Psychology for Success**

"If you give me 90% of what you call 'perfect,' we can make a profit, you can have a life, and you won't burn out. But if you keep trying to close that gap and get it '100% perfect,' you're gonna drive yourself crazy and screw things up for both of us!" - **Anonymous Senior Executive**, my first consulting firm

Years ago, when I was just starting my career with a top-notch training consulting firm as a writer and developer of training materials, I was fairly intimidated by my job and by the high-quality work of my co-workers. In response, I tried and tried to get things "perfect," putting in lots of extra hours, frustrating my family by my late evenings, and developing so much energy around my work products that I frequently engaged in long arguments defending my stuff and why it was "perfect."

The introductory quote above is from the one of the most senior executives of that company. He delivered it one evening around 7 o'clock when he found me, once again, at my desk working late. He already knew what I came to learn years later, when I was managing my own teams of training developers and media producers: **"Perfection" is a fiction… even an indulgence. There are many, many ways to get results in a project. And, rather than achieving a "perfect" result that reflects the vision of one individual, the best project teams generate results that come from collaborative, synthesized, and shared visions** – visions that meet the needs of many stakeholders and of which those many stakeholders can be proud!

Challenges...

Reflections

Reflect on these questions:
- What constitutes "perfection" for our project's outcomes? (Is this a realistic and comfortably shared vision… or an unreasonable – even arrogant – indulgence of a single team member's vision?)
- Is anyone on the project team "beating themselves up," trying to close the gap between 90% and 100% of "perfect?"
- Is someone on the project making life miserable for others by pursuing their own, idiosyncratic vision of "perfection?"

Team Challenges

Ask your team:
- What constitutes "perfect" in our deliverables? … in our customer's ultimate satisfaction?
- Are there areas where we should "dial back" our notions of perfection and maybe build rougher prototypes that aren't perfect, but would invite collaboration and help us take smaller steps toward valuable outcomes?

- In what areas of the project do you feel that we have unreasonably high expectations? What might be an alternative way to approach these areas?

Project Manager Challenges

- Review this "official" definition of project management: "... the application of knowledge, skills, tools, and techniques to project activities in order to meet or exceed stakeholder needs and expectations." So... *it's okay to meet stakeholder needs and expectations...* you don't always have to exceed them!
- Figure out ways to prove to your team that they are doing great work and that they:
  - Shouldn't drive themselves crazy trying to close the gap between 90 and 100% of perfect.
  - Are creating something that is malleable... a prototype, a work-in-progress... that will be tried and applied, with the expectation that it will be modified and improved in increments.
  - Might be indulging their unique definition of "perfect" at the exclusion of equally valid definitions of "perfect" from other stakeholders' perspectives.

Learn More...

- Read John Eliot's online article *Reverse Psychology for Success* -- http://talentdevelop.com/articles/RPFS.html

- Go to **37signals website** and **get the free online book**, *Getting Real: the Smarter, Faster, Easier Way to Build a Successful Web Application* -- https://gettingreal.37signals.com/

- Check out this *Inspired Project Teams* post: **"Think Small"** -- http://www.inspiredprojectteams.com/?p=70

- Go to **PhilosophersNotes** (http://www.philosophersnotes.com/)and get the full notes and MP3 on *Overachievement* by **John Eliot, Ph.D.**

- For related **books** and **Kindle downloads** from **Amazon.com**, go to the *Inspired Project Teams* blog post **"Let Go of Perfectionism"** and **scroll to the end of the blog post.** Direct links to related Amazon products are posted there: http://www.inspiredprojectteams.com/?p=276

Celebrate the Chaos Within

"One must still have chaos in oneself to be able to give birth to a dancing star."
- **Friedrich Nietzsche** in *Thus Spoke Zarathustra: A Book for All and None*

"All God does is watch us and kill us when we get boring. We must never, ever be boring." - **Chuck Palahniuk**

"To avoid criticism do nothing, say nothing, be nothing." - **Elbert Hubbard**

Some of the most creative people I have worked with were filled with chaos! Yet the contributions they made to our projects were frequently surprising… unique… even beautiful. Their internal chaos really could give birth to some amazing "dancing stars!"

Among my most difficult challenges as a project manager is to figure out how to handle this chaos without destroying their creativity. Early in my career, when I was too scared of losing my job to take many risks, I worked pretty hard to rein these "crazy" folks in. As the years rolled by, however, I began to look back longingly on some of the missed opportunities that these chaotic souls had pointed out to us. And I regretted not giving these people more room to move... I regretted not pushing their "wild ideas" to the limits.

So today, with the confidence of success calming my fears, I've developed this personal rule of thumb: Give these outside-the-box thinkers a little more room to move than I'm comfortable with... let them push us all (the whole team, if need be) beyond our comfort zones once in a while. And watch what happens!

Challenges...

Reflections

Reflect on these questions:
- What moments of crazy, impetuous, outside-the-box thinking have helped your projects shine?
- Have you acknowledged, praised, or even celebrated these moments of creativity?
- Are you secretly afraid that "outside the box" thinking will simply slow things up or take the project team in directions that we dare not go?

Team Challenges

Ask your team:
- What "crazy ideas" do you sometimes wish we could act on to make our product or processes better?
- How do we "sit on" or discourage outside-the-box thinking?
- What's one crazy thing you'd like to try, but have been afraid to mention for fear of looking silly or delaying the schedule?

Project Manager Challenges

- Avoid the impulse to brush aside the "crazy idea" as unrealistic. Stop and think about how it might actually work if it were modified in some minor way.
- Stay alert and vigilant for fleeting moments of wild enthusiasm for a "crazy idea."
- Celebrate divergent thinking! Praise people who have the courage to take you in strange new, but ultimately useful, directions.

Learn More...

- Check out Hugh MacLeod's How to Be Creative manifesto at the ChangeThis website. (*Caution: It's R-Rated!*) -- http://www.changethis.com/6.HowToBeCreative

- Go to PhilosophersNotes (http://www.philosophersnotes.com/) and get the full notes and MP3 on Friedrich Nietzsche's **Thus Spoke Zarathustra**.

- Get the 4 Disc CD set or audio download of Thus Spoke Zarathustra, narrated by Alex Jennings, from LearnOutLoud.com. -- http://www.learnoutloud.com/Product/T018118/81719

- For related **books** and **Kindle downloads** from **Amazon.com**, go to the *Inspired Project Teams* blog post **"Celebrate the Chaos Within"** and **scroll to the end of the blog post.** Direct links to related Amazon products are posted there: http://www.inspiredprojectteams.com/?p=297

Embrace the Work Itself

Projects are the most goal-oriented of human endeavors. And if you spend most of your life working on projects, as so many of our project team members do, **you can develop an uneasy, ever-present sense that you are never really finished.** There's a continual nagging feeling that you've not completed your work because the next goal is endlessly popping up in front of you, demanding your attention.

So where's the joy in the work itself? What about the intrinsic value of our chosen profession? The beauty and fascination of the field itself? **What about the practice of our profession?**

Consider this from **George Leonard's *Mastery: The Keys to Success and Long-Term Fulfillment*** (my bold added for emphasis):

> "Goals and contingencies... are important. But they exist in the future and the past, beyond the pale of the sensory realm. **Practice, the path of mastery, exists only in the present. You can see it, hear it, smell it, feel it. To love the plateau is to love the eternal now**, to enjoy the inevitable spurts of progress and the fruits of accomplishment, then serenely to accept the new plateau that waits just beyond them. To love the plateau is to love what is most essential and enduring..."

Challenges...

Reflections

Reflect on these questions:
- What's so great about your chosen profession? Why did you choose it?
- What is it about the "doing" of your work that brings you joy?

Team Challenges

Ask your team:
- What attracted you to your profession? Why did you choose it?
- What fascinates, satisfies, fulfills you about the work itself?
- When you "lose track of time" and disappear into your work, what tasks are you performing?

Project Manager Challenges
- Observe your project team members and try to see what's going on when they are "flowing" or completely engaged in their work.
- Find the quiet joy that keeps them going. Let yourself be amazed at their inspirations.
- Honestly express your appreciation so they know that you know they are doing wonderful things.

Learn More...

- Go to PhilosophersNotes (http://www.philosophersnotes.com/) and get the full notes and MP3 on *Mastery* by George Leonard.

- For related books and Kindle downloads from Amazon.com, go to the *Inspired Project Teams blog post* **"Embrace the Work Itself"** and scroll to the end of the blog post. Direct links to related Amazon products are posted there: http://www.inspiredprojectteams.com/?p=265

Take the Risk

This post is all about getting outside your comfort zone. It's about encouraging you to run with open arms to embrace that somewhat scary opportunity that you see in front of you. **If you can imagine it... if you can see it clearly... if it gets you excited as a possibility, then it may be your destiny to make it a reality.** As **Ralph Waldo Emerson** says: "There's nothing capricious in nature, and the implanting of a desire indicates that its gratification is in the constitution of the creature that feels it." In other words, the very fact that you can imagine a new path or a new invention or a new way of being indicates that it is part of your larger life's purpose to manifest it.

Emerson elaborates:
"Our desires presage the capacities within us; they are harbingers of what we shall be able to accomplish. What we can do and want to do is projected in our imagination, quite outside ourselves, and into the future. We are attracted to what is already ours in secret. Thus passionate anticipation transforms what is indeed possible into dreamt-for reality."
- from ***The Selected Writings of Ralph Waldo Emerson***

The point: If you are imagining it and you feel excitement (and possibly a little fear) about making it real, then you should probably take the risk and go for it! As Emerson says: "God will not have his work made manifest by cowards." Similar words of encouragement are captured by **Joseph Campbell** in his book, ***A Joseph Campbell Companion***. Campbell tells us:

"A bit of advice given to a young Native American at the time of his initiation: 'As you go the way of life, you will see a great chasm. Jump. It's not as wide as you think.'"

What's more, as anyone who's leaped across chasms will tell you, the more leaps you make, the more fearless and confident you will become. Soon, the chasms will seem narrower and you'll look forward to the opportunity to jump!

Three Good Reasons to Take That Risk

Now, from the perspective of several decades as a working professional, I can see at least three good reasons to take that risk and to make a few mistakes along the way.

Reason 1. You'll grow.

As **Henry C. Link** tells us: "While one person hesitates because he feels inferior, the other is busy making mistakes and becoming superior." Then there's this from Joseph Campbell: "The old skin has to be shed before the new one can come." And finally, **Tony Robbins** says: "Success is the result of good judgment, good judgment is a result of experience, experience is often the result of bad judgment." (From **Brian Johnson's PhilosophersNotes website**.) So make your mistakes, shed that old skin, and make a few bad judgments. Without these, you simply can't grow!

Reason 2. You'll create something new or amazing.

Most new or amazing creations are the result of someone taking the risk to pursue them. As Brian Johnson tells us in his **PhilosophersNote on Psycho-Cybernetics**: "It took **Edison** 10,000 'failures' to figure out the light bulb. [Edison] said: 'I have not failed. I've just found 10,000 ways that won't work.'"

And recently **researchers at a US Navy laboratory** have unveiled what they say is significant evidence of **cold fusion**, a potentially cheap, limitless and environmentally-clean source of energy. What's more, it appears that some of the same scientists who have been laughed at for decades and risked their careers by pursuing cold fusion as an impossible dream may have been responsible, in part, for these recent breakthroughs. And who knows? Someday soon, we could all benefit from their risky leap across the chasm!

Reason 3. You'll become inspired, connect with your Source, your God, or the universe, and acquire new energy.

There's something about accepting the challenge of a dream that seems to open a channel to the divine within us. When we say "Yes" to stepping outside our comfort zone and pursuing a great dream, energy from Source or God or the universe seems to flow in to support us and keep us working. As **Paulo Coelho** says in his novel **Veronika Decides to Die**: "Live. If you live, God will live with you. If you refuse to run his risks, he'll retreat to that distant heaven and be merely a subject for philosophical speculation. Everyone knows this, but no one takes the first step, perhaps for fear of being called insane."

So take the risk, become more inspired, and surf on the wave of Source energy that follows. And remember this from **William James**: "Most people never run far enough on their first wind to find out they've got a second. Give your dreams all you've got and you'll be amazed at the energy that comes out of you." (From Brian Johnson's PhilosophersNotes website.) **The object of the game: Take the risk, give it all you've got, and watch the universe conspire with you to help you** achieve your dreams!

Two Personal Examples of Risk Taking

I know from personal experience that taking a risk and going after a scary, almost unimaginable possibility can be transformative. There are at least two situations in which accepting the risk has led me to a whole new dimension in my professional life.

The first situation, and absolutely the most frightening, was **when I walked away from a steady paycheck to become an independent consultant.**

Here's the story. I had a whopping four years of experience in the business world working for a consulting firm, most of which was spent having an aggressive sales team sell the services of us instructional development consultants to clients such as IBM, Xerox, Honeywell, and other major corporations. It was exciting work and I loved it and learned a lot. Trouble was, a major publishing house (filled with editors and book sales people) acquired this consulting firm and promptly began messing with its business model, driving most of us crazy by challenging our professional standards and practices.

As you might imagine, people were jumping ship left and right, leaving to establish their own independent consulting practices. They generally made lots more money, worked their own hours, and had the thrill of charting their own course in the world. I really envied them and was tempted to follow their lead! However, most of these folks were single and were traveling through life fairly unencumbered. In contrast, I had a wife, two school-aged kids and a two-year-old mortgage on our first-ever home in sunny, but expensive, Southern California. If I went independent, I'd lose that steady paycheck. And if I couldn't find enough contracts, I could lose the house and the ability to support my family. Talk about risk!

Fortunately, my wife really believed in me. She encouraged me, told me she'd use her financial and math training to handle the fiscal side of things, and generally pushed me to jump across that chasm to our own independent business. As I sit here writing this, I look up on the wall and see a copy of **my Declaration of Professional Independence** (framed and dated) presented to her on her birthday shortly after we began talking about this dream.

Over the next decade, we built a network of sub-contractors and media producers and worked with major corporate clients to develop award-winning, custom training programs. We paid off our house and were able to become much more financially secure than had I stayed with the consulting firm. What's more, with the experience I gained managing projects and teams, I eventually began to move into writing books about project management and teaching PM workshops. In short, taking what appeared to be a huge risk and following my dream, I completely transformed my professional life, as well as the quality of life for my family.

My second example of professional risk taking is my *Inspired Project Teams* blog and podcast. My career had so far been all about achieving observable results in the human performance arena. I belonged to a profession that actually refers to itself as HPT people (Human Performance Technologists) and whose members carefully design instructional experiences so that people can acquire observable, measureable skills. I have a solid, decades-long track record helping clients achieve results through systematic HPT and instructional design practices and through my skill-based project management workshops. Then along came Brian Johnson and his **PhilosophersNotes**.

In the past year or so, listening daily during my workouts, I have been exposed to hundreds of Brian's "big ideas" that began to work their way into my consciousness. The result: I became filled with a passion to share with the world all the ways that these big ideas could inspire project teams and project managers to achieve their best. Now these days my former HPT, performance-measuring self is watching me work on all these "inspirational" posts and podcasts and is shaking his head in wonder, a little dismayed. The question my former self keeps asking me is: "So how do you measure inspiration? How can you know this stuff will do anyone any good!"

Truth is, I have no answer to this. I just know that somewhere deep inside there is a voice pushing me and assuring me that this is important work. And, in a tip of the hat to my HPT colleagues, I have been carefully providing Challenges with each post that gently encourage you, dear reader, to apply (put into practice) these inspirational ideas in your workplace or in your life.

So it's quite possible that this blog could lead to people acquiring solid new (even measurable!?) skills. In any event, I realize that my focus on something as intangible as "inspiration" runs the risk that I will be regarded as working with fluffy, "new age" ideas. And this ultimately means I could be risking my hard-won reputation in the HPT world! Well then... so be it! I have made the leap and I eagerly await whatever is on the other side of this chasm!

So... What If You Make a Mistake?

Repeatedly as I've studied this topic of risk, I hear this message: Don't panic if you screw up! Just accept it and move on. In **Psycho-Cybernetics: A New Technique for Using Your Subconscious Power**, **Maxwell Maltz** says: "The great **Babe Ruth**, who holds the record for the most home runs, also holds the record for the most strike-outs. It is in the nature of things that we progress by acting, making mistakes, and correcting course."

Then there's this from Ralph Waldo Emerson's essay, **Self-Reliance**: "The voyage of the best ship is a zigzag line of a hundred tacks. See the line from a sufficient distance, and it straightens itself to the average tendency." So you need not panic when you are in one of those seemingly off-course zigs or zags! Just step back, look at the big picture and you're likely to see that, overall, you are moving toward your destination.

So take the risk. Leap across the chasm. Screw up and learn and correct your course and leap again! It's all part of your journey.

Challenges...

Reflections

Reflect on these questions:
- Is our project team overly cautious?
- When's the last time we laughed nervously as co-consipirators or got a little apprehensive about a potentially strange or unlikely solution to a problem?
- When's the last time we got really excited about an completely innovative solution to a problem?
- What might we do to be more creative... to take a few more risks?

Team Challenges

Ask your team:
- If there were no consequences whatsoever, and you could do anything or try anything, what would you do or try?
- Are the consequences that you imagine real?
- How might you mitigate these consequences? Or eliminate them entirely?
- Is there really anything stopping you from taking a chance on this? How could you challenge that which is stopping you?
- Could you try a prototype or test of your idea to see if it's really all that risky?

Project Manager Challenges

- Practice true brainstorming with your team... no judgments, no criticisms, just free-wheeling, outside-the-box thinking and "making stuff up." Gently encourage risk taking.
- In casual conversations, when team members come up with "off the wall" ideas, withhold judgment. Pause, think about the ideas, let them "marinate." Encourage them, keep thinking about the ideas, and (really!) return to them later.
- Synthesize! Try listing as many features as you can of the wild or seemingly risky solutions. Then, bang this list of features up against the more "practical" solutions and keep the best features of both the risky and the practical solutions.

Learn More...

- Go to **PhilosophersNotes** (http://www.philosophersnotes.com/) and get the full notes and MP3s on:
    - Ralph Waldo Emerson's *The Selected Writings of Ralph Waldo Emerson*
    - Ralph Waldo Emerson's *Self-Reliance: The Classic Essay on Trusting Yourself*
    - *A Joseph Campbell Companion: Reflections on the Art of Living*
    - *Psycho-Cybernetics: A New Technique for Using Your Subconscious Power*
    - *Paulo Coelho: A Look at Some of My Favorite Big Ideas*
    - *Notes on Tony Robbins*

- Get the **Essential Emerson CD, narrated by Archibald Macleish**, from **LearnOutLoud.com**. -- http://www.learnoutloud.com/Product/E028499/81719

- Get the 6 hour **Joseph Campbell and the Power of Myth CD** narrated by Joseph Campbell & Bill Moyers from **LearnOutLoud.com**.-- http://www.learnoutloud.com/Product/J003295/81719

- Get the 4 hour **The Alchemist by Paulo Coelho CD** narrated by Jeremy Irons from **LearnOutLoud.com** -- http://www.learnoutloud.com/Product/T020699/81719

- Get the 1 hour **The Higher Reaches of Success: Understanding What Drives People CD** narrated by Tony Robbins & Ken Wilbur from **LearnOutLoud.com** – http://www.learnoutloud.com/Product/T021088/81719

- For related books and Kindle downloads from Amazon.com, go to the *Inspired Project Teams* blog post "**Take the Risk**" and scroll to the end of the blog post. Direct links to related Amazon products are posted there: http://www.inspiredprojectteams.com/?p=779

Just Say No

In most of these Inspired Project Teams posts and podcasts, I've tried to focus on the positive. We've examined optimism, happiness, trusting your inner voice, embracing your work, joyfully taking risks, and generally saying "yes!" to the challenges you and your team face. However, **while it might make sense for individuals to say "yes" to life as often as they can, there are critical moments when project teams have just gotta say "no!"** Otherwise, your team could find itself swamped by chores that you never agreed to and that are not tied to the essential project deliverables.

As Stephen Covey says:
"You have to decide what your highest priorities are and have the courage—pleasantly, smilingly, non-apologetically, to say 'no' to other things. And the way you do that is by having a bigger 'yes' burning inside. The enemy of the 'best' is often the 'good.'" – **Stephen Covey** in *The 7 Habits of Highly Effective People*.

Then there's this from journalist **Herbert Bayard Swope**:

"I can't give you a sure-fire formula for success, but I can give you a formula for failure: try to please everybody all the time."

Finally, **Steve Jobs** warns:

"You can't just ask customers what they want and then try to give that to them. By the time you get it built, they'll want something new."

Be the Plumber

The best people – the ones you really want on your team – are highly-motivated professionals who want to do great work. That's the good news. The bad news is that these same highly motivated people often find it difficult to say "no" to add-ons, those additional bells-and-whistles that customers and stakeholders dream up as "nice to have." Each request for add-ons poses a challenge to these high achievers. For them, meeting and beating that challenge can often be a matter of personal pride. Unfortunately, most project budgets are finite, as are project schedules. So adding deliverables – even ones that are professionally challenging and potentially wonderful — usually means chewing up more time and money than is available.

In my classes I challenge new project managers to "be the plumber." That is, to ask yourself this question: What would happen if you contracted with a plumber to put new plumbing in your kitchen and then, half-way through the project, ask him to add new plumbing for a nearby bathroom? Everyone realizes that doesn't make sense! Either the plumber would say "no" flat out, or he would demand two essentials to accept such a request: more time and more money!

But for some odd reason, many professionals find the plumber's simple business logic difficult to grasp. I'm guessing this is largely due to grad school habits and internship experiences in which they gleefully accepted every challenge and request that came from advisers or supervisors. And if this meant working around the clock, accepting unfair assignments and changes, or generally allowing themselves to be the victims, then so be it. That was all part of the hazing … er… challenge of earning a place in their chosen profession. The result: By the time they are employed in our organizations, they've had plenty of practice having people ask them to do more or provide additional features, without offering more time or money, and they readily agree because doing so has become a habit! The original contract, the original project specifications, even the original verbal agreements everyone supported can be forgotten as these seemingly reasonable requests for "little add-ons" or enhancements are accepted. And later, when the project budget and schedule are blown, the whole project team is blamed.

So here's the deal: Our project teams need to say "no" to such requests… as Covey says, "smilingly, non-apologetically" — but "no!" And that means drawing on that strength that comes from having that bigger "yes" that burns within. That bigger "yes" that is the unique definition of quality deriving from the team's shared passion for the limited and finite project vision that everyone agreed to in the first place!

Senior Managers and Customers Respect a Well-Reasoned "No"

Finally, here's a footnote for all of you who are thinking that saying "no" is going to get you in trouble with your clients or senior management. During the debriefing sessions following my PM Basics workshops, I ask my class participants to develop a list of organizational changes they'd like to see made in order for them to improve their project management practices or the way things are done in the organization. Invariably, the recommendation "Reduce the workload or get us more people to help us" ends up on these lists. At the end of these debriefing sessions, I ask the participants' senior managers to join us and hear what the class is recommending. Class participants wait nervously to hear what the big bosses are going to say when they hear the "less work or more people" suggestion. And almost always they're pleasantly surprised to hear the response. Invariably senior managers respond with something like this: "Well, why didn't you tell us your workload was too much? Unless we hear differently, we're going to assume that you have all the people you need. So from now on, speak up! Otherwise we'll just keep piling on the work!"

The lesson that's learned from this response: Take a deep breath, summon your courage, and just say "no." For the sake of quality… for the sake of that bigger "yes" burning inside… Just say "no." Your senior managers, customers, and project sponsors will respect you for it.

Challenges…

Reflections

Reflect on these questions:
- Are there elements of our project that might be vulnerable to "scope creep" from our stakeholders' expanding "wish lists?"
- Are team members prepared to say "no" to these wish lists "smilingly, nonapologetically?"
- Are any of your team members predisposed to saying "Yes" to certain enhancements that they would enjoy creating, but that aren't part of the project

specifications? Are you staying alert to these potential scope changes and figuring out the best ways to handle them?

Team Challenges

Ask your team:
- What are some parts of our project that might be vulnerable to "scope creep" from stakeholders' wish lists?
- How will you handle these requests for add-ons?
- What do you need from me (as project manager or team leader)… or from other people inside or outside the project team that would help you say "no" more confidently to these add-on requests?

Project Manager Challenges

- Make sure everyone on the project team has deep knowledge and respect for the boundaries of the project. Make sure they know, and are willing to defend, the finite nature of the project deliverables as specified in the contract or the work plan.
- If you haven't already done so, make sure there is a method in place for handling add-ons, wishes, and other requests for expanding the project scope. For example: Keep a list of items marked "Version 2" or "Enhancements for Future Projects" when you're in those meetings with stakeholders. These items can be rolled into another, subsequent project that is separately funded and has its own schedule. That way stakeholders are assured that their ideas are captured.
- Back up your team members and be there to help them say "No" when they are faced with scope creep.

Learn More...

- Check out this related ***Inspired Project Teams*** post/podcast: **Spend More Time in Quadrant 2** -- http://www.inspiredprojectteams.com/?p=544

- Go to **PhilosophersNotes** (http://www.philosophersnotes.com/) and **get the full notes and MP3 on *The 7 Habits of Highly Effective People*** by Stephen Covey.

- Get the ***12 hrs. 58 min. unabridged audio edition of* <u>The 7 Habits of Highly Effective People</u>**, narrated by the author, Stephen Covey, from **LearnOutLoud.com** -- http://www.learnoutloud.com/Product/T015594/81719

- For related books and Kindle downloads from Amazon.com, go to the *Inspired Project Teams* blog post "***Just Say No***" and scroll to the end of the blog post. Direct links to related Amazon products are posted there: http://www.inspiredprojectteams.com/?p=944

- Go to **FranklinCovey.com** for lots of great information on new books and other resources by Stephen Covey. -- http://www.franklincovey.com/

Listen, Understand, Collaborate

"Habit 5: Seek First to Understand, Then to be Understood." – **Stephen Covey** in *The Seven Habits of Highly Effective People*

"Knowledge speaks, but wisdom listens."- **Jimi Hendrix**

Professionals… especially the energetic, creative people you want on your project teams… can sometimes develop a mental image of themselves as essentially knights in shining armor, riding in to save the day! Unfortunately, this can sometimes mean that they jump to conclusions too quickly, seeking little input and assuming that the problem to be solved is just like one they solved the week before.

On the other hand, the best professionals employ a more consultative mental model: They see themselves as creative solvers of unique, challenging problems. They listen, question, and try to understand the customer's needs. They test their understanding by rephrasing the customer's statements. Then they formulate one or more potential solutions and present them carefully. In short, they "seek first to understand, then to be understood."

Challenges…

Reflections

Reflect on these questions:
- Have there been times when our team has "jumped the gun" and rushed to judgment without getting all the facts?
- Do we set aside time throughout the project to thoughtfully discuss our customers' opinions about our work or our deliverables as they are evolving?
- Do we spend enough time actively listening (and rephrasing to show our understanding)?
- Do some team members avoid customer contact because it's difficult (or frustrating) to listen to them? If so, how might we address this problem?

Team Challenges

Ask your team:

- Under what circumstances is it difficult to spend time listening to customers?
- When was the last time you secretly wanted to hang up the phone or walk out of the room in the middle of a discussion with a customer? What could you do to avoid this situation in the future?
- How can we get better-quality input from our customers?
- What should we do (what kind of meeting or forum could we structure) to encourage our customers to provide high-quality input that we can really use?

Project Manager Challenges

- Make sure your project schedules allow for plenty of incremental input from reviewers and customers as the deliverables are evolving. (Consider formal "mini-reviews" of several iterations of the deliverables… i.e., concept papers, drafts, prototypes, test versions, final deliverables, etc.)
- Observe project team members when they interact with customers. Ask yourself these questions:
  - Are they really "getting" what the customers are trying to say?
  - Are they actively listening and rephrasing to check their understanding?
  - Is our jargon or the customer's jargon adequately translated so that each party understands what the other is trying to say?
  - Is anyone "rushing to judgment" before all the information is in?
  - Do team members truly empathize with the customer's position? … their frustrations and fears?
- Make clear notes regarding any "sticking points" or areas of disagreement you observed, along with specific examples of the exact dialogue you observed among all parties. (Consider video or audio recording for later analysis, if the communication issues are particularly serious.)
- Brainstorm with the team members involved to come up with some suggestions for avoiding these communication difficulties in the future.

Learn More…

- Go to **PhilosophersNotes** (http://www.philosophersnotes.com/) and get the full notes and MP3 on *The Seven Habits of Highly Effective People*

- Get the *full, 13-hour audio of The Seven Habits of Highly Effective People*, narrated by Stephen Covey, from **LearnOutLoud.com** -- http://www.learnoutloud.com/Product/T015594/81719

- For related books and Kindle downloads from Amazon.com, go to the *Inspired Project Teams* blog post **"Listen, Understand, Collaborate"** and scroll to the end of the blog post. Direct links to related Amazon products are posted there: http://www.inspiredprojectteams.com/?p=191

- Go to **FranklinCovey.com** for lots of great information on new books and other resources by Stephen Covey. -- http://www.franklincovey.com/

Just Do It!

It is my intent in this post to convince you of the tremendous liberating power of simply taking action. **I want to encourage you to get moving… to get unstuck… to just do it!** If you and your project team members are sometimes plagued with fits of analysis paralysis or procrastination, accompanied by worry over all the bad things that might happen when you take action, then this post (podcast) is for you.

Let's start with a couple of powerful quotes:

"A good idea if not acted upon produces terrible psychological pain. But a good idea acted upon brings enormous mental satisfaction. Got a good idea? Then do something about it. Use action to cure fear and gain confidence. Here's something to remember: Actions feed and strengthen confidence; inaction in all forms feeds fear. To fight fear, act. To increase fear — wait, put off, postpone… Jot that down in your success rule book right now. Action cures fear." – **David J. Schwartz** in *The Magic of Thinking Big*.

Think about it. What Schwartz says makes sense! How often have you spent days and days putting off an action because you feared some dire consequences, only to find out later (after you acted) that these consequences were simply not real! In the meantime, for days, you lived through the agony of dreading your negative fantasy!

So… you say you know what to do, but are just feeling hesitant about it? Maybe you've convinced yourself that you need to do "a little more homework" before you get started. Okay. It's always good to think through a problem before you act. But remember this from **Dale Carnegie** in *How to Stop Worrying and Start Living*: "… knowledge isn't power until it is applied; [my] purpose …is to remind you of what you already know and to kick you in the shins and inspire you to do something about applying it." Carnegie also says: "Spit on your hands and get busy. Your blood will start circulating; your mind will start ticking–and pretty soon this whole positive upsurge of life in your body will drive worry from your mind. Get busy. Keep busy."

Castor Beans and Procrastination

Here's an example of how I've let procrastination ruin my own peace of mind: In Southern California where I live, castor beans are to the plant world what cockroaches are to the insect world. They are invasive, extremely aggressive about staying alive and procreating, and almost impossible to eliminate once they get a foothold on your property. They produce large, ugly leaves; choke out everything near them; and soon tower 8 or 10 feet over the yard like some kind of berserk bamboo colony, dropping spiny, barbed, and poisonous seeds that hit the ground and immediately go to work adding more plants to the colony! Now just behind the fence at the back of our beautiful, did-it-ourselves, landscaped back yard is an easement separating our property from our neighbor's. Here, secluded from the view of both property owners, those sneaky castor bean plants sprout, grow, and gather momentum. Left unchecked, like we did one year when we left town for a several months, these guys can grow taller than the people who have to battle them. And once they get a few feet tall, they extend their tough roots deep into the ground. Removing them when they have grown even moderately large is a huge chore requiring a lot of cutting and digging and much scratching of forearms and hands.

So everyone knows that the best way to deal with these things is to get them while they're young, digging them out when they are small plants. And when you're done, you can't assume they're gone for good. You have to check on them frequently because the seeds from an ancient crop that was allowed to go unchecked several years ago can lie in wait and spring to life when you least expect it.

Now I love sitting in my yard and enjoying a cup of coffee in the morning. My wife's carefully staged flower plantings produce beautiful changing displays as one type of flower passes its prime and another begins blooming. And I love watching the bees, hummingbirds and finches work the blooms while the mockingbird sings his amazing melodies to lure a mate. It's truly a peaceful place of renewal.

Temporarily peaceful, that is… until I see, through the cracks between the fence slats, the little green castor bean plants bobbing in the sunshine. Then I groan, knowing what's in store for me. Getting rid of these things will take two ladders (one for my side of the fence and one hoisted over to the other side to get me down into the easement), moving some of the neighbor's junk that he keeps throwing back there, then cutting the plants and digging out the root systems, and finally getting all the debris back over the fence and into the recycle bins. In other words, the whole process is a pain!

So I look away. I watch my pretty flowers and birds, and I try to put this nasty, but necessary, chore out of my mind. Unfortunately, it doesn't work. Now that I have spotted them, the irritating little plants sway in the breeze, peeking through the fence slats and taunt me. This goes on for several days. Each of my coffee breaks begins with peacefully enjoying the flowers and birds, then quickly turns to an annoying strain as I try to force myself to ignore the growing bean plants. Eventually, I assemble my tools and ladders and tackle the chore of removing these pests. But not before I've allowed them to spoil my coffee break for days on end. A couple of hours work… a couple hours of "just do it"… would have finished the job. And that would have given me my peaceful coffee breaks a lot sooner.

Don't Wait: Do It Now!

Now I realize that when you're working with a project team, taking action can be a lot more complicated than removing weeds. On one of my project teams, for example, I had a writer who absolutely drove the client crazy. This person had two grad school degrees, plenty of publications to his credit, and a stellar track record… on paper. Unfortunately his one-on-one communications skills were terrible! With clients (especially women, for some reason) he was impatient, arrogant, abrasive, and sometimes flat out obstinent.

Trouble was, by the time I found out how unbearably he was behaving with our female client, he had completed the research and a preliminary outline for the project component he had been assigned. If I were to fire him, a lot of time would be lost. So, I prolonged the agony by accompanying him on every meeting with the client and "keeping him in line" as best I could. Eventually the client reached her limit, as did I, and I replaced this guy with a kinder, gentler writer. True, it caused a delay in the project as the new person got up to speed. But the new person's enthusiasm and the good will extended him by the client changed the whole atmosphere of the project.

The bottom line: We all suffered more than we had to, because I didn't "just do it" earlier! (And, by the way, that obnoxious writer I fired found himself a position working pretty much alone with "no one looking over his shoulder" as he put it. So even he benefited from the change!)

As **Russell Simmons** says in his book, ***Do You!***:

"Stalling leads to sickness. But taking steps, even baby steps, always leads to success."

Sounds good. But sometimes, especially when the situation you are facing is complex, it can be extremely difficult to get unstuck and take action. If you find yourself stuck, consider these **specific recommendations for getting moving from Dale Carnegie:**

"Experience has proved to me, time after time, the enormous value of arriving at a decision. It is the failure to arrive at a fixed purpose, the inability to stop going around and round in maddening circles, that drives men to nervous breakdowns and living hells. I find that fifty per cent of my worries vanishes once I arrive at a clear, definite decision; and another forty per cent usually vanishes once I start to carry out that decision.

So, **I banish about 90 per cent of my worries by taking these four steps**:
1. Writing down precisely what I am worried about.
2. Writing down what I can do about it.
3. Deciding what to do.
4. Starting immediately to carry out that decision."

This is a brilliant approach! And it addresses the demands of even the most analytical among us, because it uses a logical, systematic series of steps. The key, however, is that you "just do it!" You need to actually take these steps!

As Dr. Phil tells us in his **Life Law #5: "Life rewards action.** [You need to] make careful decisions and then pull the trigger. Learn that the world couldn't care less about thoughts without actions." (From **Dr. Phil McGraw's *Life Strategies: Doing What Works, Doing What Matters***)

And so what if you make a mistake? We learn from mistakes. In fact, we can't learn anything without making mistakes. As **Ralph Waldo Emerson says**, "All life is an experiment. The more experiments you make the better."

So no matter what, we need to keep moving… we must take action. In the words of **Calvin Coolidge**:

"Nothing in the world can take the place of persistence. Talent will not; nothing is more common than unsuccessful men with talent. Genius will not; unrewarded genius is almost a proverb. Education will not; the world is full of educated derelicts. Persistence and determination are omnipotent. The slogan 'press on' has solved and always will solve the problems of the human race."

So get out there and "just do it!"

Challenges...

Reflections

Reflect on these questions:
- Looking back, have you ever been "stuck" when working on a project? How did you get unstuck? If fear was involved, how did you overcome it?
- Is there someone on your project team who is:
  - suffering from analysis paralysis?
  - waiting, afraid to take action, until they get that special input from that special person?
  - just plain scared to take action until all the conditions are "perfect?"
- Have other people in your organization ever been similarly immobilized? How did they get unstuck and move on?

Team Challenges

Ask your team:
- In what areas of this project are you feeling stuck?
- Which project tasks are you most afraid of working on or most afraid of completing in an unsatisfactory form?
- What specific help, support, encouragement, or resources do you need to overcome these fears and to get unstuck?
- Which project tasks are you most likely to put off doing... Which ones are you most likely to procrastinate in completing?
- What one thing could senior management or project management or the customer/client provide that would get you moving and keep you moving?
- What's preventing you from asking for this?

Project Manager Challenges

- Think about the responses to the previous Reflections and Team Challenges. Make a "to do" list of things you should be doing to eliminate the factors that are preventing the project team members from "just doing it."
- Think about Dale Carnegie's four-step process for banishing worry and indecision and for stimulating action.
- Create a worksheet titled "Just Do It: Banish Worry" that presents a modified version of Carnegie's four steps listed as follows:
  - 1. Precisely what are you worried about? [Be specific.]
  - 2. What can you do about this thing that worries you? [Make a list of options. Be specific.]
  - 3. Decide what to do. [Choose among the options.]
  - 4. Take action. Now!
- Sit down with anyone on your team who is stuck and who should be taking action. Introduce them to the "Just Do It: Banish Worry" worksheet and help them use this tool to get moving on their project and "just do it!"
- If it makes sense, consider having "stuck" project team members work out of sequence, start in the middle, go help someone who's already got momentum try

building a prototype or outline or do anything concrete and engaging that will help them turn their worries into action.

Learn More…

- Go to PhilosophersNotes (http://www.philosophersnotes.com/) and download the full notes and MP3 versions of the following books:
  - *The Magic of Thinking Big* – David J. Schwartz
  - Dale Carnegie's *How to Stop Worrying and Start Living*
  - Russell Simmons' *Do You!*
  - The Selected Writings of Ralph Waldo Emerson

- Get the **four-hour audio** of David Schwartz's ***The Magic of Thinking Big*** from **Learn Out Loud.com** -- http://www.learnoutloud.com/Product/T002276/81719

- Get the **10 hr 15 min unabridged audio** of Dale Carnegie's ***How to Stop Worrying and Start Living*** from **Learn out loud .com** -- http://www.learnoutloud.com/Product/H019841/81719

- Get the abridged **audio** version (narrated by the author) of Dr. Phil McGraw's ***Life Strategies: Doing What Works, Doing What Matters*** from **LearnOutLoud.com** -- http://www.learnoutloud.com/Product/L005006/81719

- For related books and Kindle downloads from Amazon.com, go to the *Inspired Project Teams* blog post **"Just Do It!"** and scroll to the end of the blog post. Direct links to related Amazon products are posted there: http://www.inspiredprojectteams.com/?p=724

Consciously Choose Your Attitude

Your attitude is that collection of feelings that you bring to a situation or to a relationship. If the prevailing attitude of your project team is negative, cynical, or hopeless, then there's a good chance your project results and work processes will reflect that bad energy. On the other hand, if you and your team feel positive and enthusiastic, then you're likely to have a better work experience and produce higher quality work products. So **a project team's attitude can make or break the project.** But what can you do about something as intangible as your attitude?

In this post I hope to show you how you can consciously choose your attitude instead of simply allowing it to overtake you as a collection of random feelings. And when you bring consciousness to your attitude, you can change the very texture of your life. Ultimately, it's up to you whether you live in darkness or light, in a field of crackling tension or a glow of enthusiastic energy.

Some Quotations to Illustrate

Here are some powerful quotes to illustrate. The first is from Victor Frankl, a man who was stripped of everything as he witnessed his family abused, tortured, and killed by their Nazi captors. Enduring incredible miseries, he was ultimately led to this realization:

> "…Everything can be taken from a man but one thing; the last of the human freedoms -- to choose one's attitude in any given set of circumstances, to choose one's own way."
> - **Viktor Frankl** in *Man's Search for Meaning*

Then there's this from **Marcus Aurelius** in his ***Meditations***:

"If you are distressed by anything external, the pain is not due to the thing itself but to your own estimate of it; and this you have the power to revoke at any moment."

Finally, Greek Stoic philosopher **Epictetus** writes in ***The Enchiridion***:

"We cannot choose our external circumstances, but we can always choose how we respond to them."

The message of these and many other great philosophers and teachers is this: **We have the power to choose our attitudes.** But how can we apply this message in our everyday lives?

Some Examples: The Lineman, The Farmer, The Trucker, & The Storm Chaser

Consider these examples. I'm standing outside on a typical summer day. Off on the distant horizon, I see a wall of huge, dark clouds forming. There is a thick breeze and a slight smell of wetness and ozone in the air. The sun disappears. I hear a far-off rumble. Now, if ever there was an external event that speaks to my ancient lizard brain, it's this approaching storm. A sense of anticipation wells up within me… even excitement. What will this storm bring?

For purposes of this discussion, a better question might be: What attitude do I bring to this storm? As the son of **an electric company lineman**, I feel myself anticipating the destructive forces of the lightning and thunder and winds that so often took my father out with his crews when power lines were knocked down, leaving hospitals and supermarkets and ordinary homeowners without the electricity they depended upon. So I might recall and begin to feel the fear of a kid who is hoping his father is going to return home safely after he battles the elements.

On the other hand, I might have the more hopeful attitude of some of my Pennsylvania **farmer** neighbors who, let's say, have been enduring a long drought and have been watching their crops wither without life-giving rains. For these folks, the attitude that manifests is more likely to be eager anticipation or even enthusiasm. They are hoping the rain will renew their crops and save them from financial loss.

Then there's **the long-haul trucker**, speeding down a highway that disappears into this storm on a mission to deliver his load on schedule. He's seen lots of big rigs overturned by similar storms, so his attitude is one of cautious calculation (maybe even a little frustration), as he tries to figure out how much risk the storm poses and whether he should keep moving, change his route, or simply park some place and let the storm pass.

Finally, there is **the storm chaser** whose goal is to photograph the amazing natural forces unleashed by such storms. Seeing the thunderheads gather, her attitude is one of eager anticipation as she scans the horizon for that next opportunity to capture a breath-taking photo.

Here's the point: **The storm is a neutral event.** A meteorologist could simply define it in terms of the natural forces that are converging to create it. The individuals experiencing this storm, however, bring to it their own values, dreams, hopes, and trepidations. Whether they experience it as an object of fear, a welcome event, or a nuisance to be dealt with depends entirely on their choice of attitude. And we all have the power to choose any attitude. **We have the power to give the external event any meaning.**

Bring Your Own Meaning…

As **Brian Johnson** says in his **PhilosphersNotes** on *The Diamond Cutter*, by **Geshe Michael Roach** :

"NOTHING has meaning outside of that which we give it. Nothing has any *absolute* meaning because, if it did, then EVERYONE would experience it EXACTLY the same, ALL THE TIME. Everything, as the Buddhists say, is 'empty' of meaning."

So… **it's what you bring to the world that determines your experience of it.** This means that if you think your life or your relationship or your world is a mess, then you are most likely choosing to put the pieces of your puzzle together in such a way as to support your thesis that life is a mess. Remember, even Victor Frankl, after suffering incredible torture and abuse, found tremendous power in his discovery that he had the ability to choose his attitude. He didn't need to feel defeated. He could instead feel his freedom to choose.

And, ultimately, this freedom to choose our attitude and choose our response can have a huge impact on our overall happiness. Consider this from **Marci Shimoff**'s book *Happy for No Reason: 7 Steps to Being Happy from the Inside Out:*

"Our ability to respond to what happens to us–our response-ability–dramatically affects our happiness. [Happy people] respond to the events in their lives in a way that supports their inner peace and well-being."

So the choice is yours: You can choose to describe your world and external events from an attitude that is negative and grim. Or you can choose an attitude that supports positive engagement, positive outcomes, and a generally positive state of mind.

A PM Example: A Day at the Races…

Here's an example from my own project management experience that illustrates how an entire team can choose a positive attitude in questionable circumstances. A while back, I was managing a team that was producing a large sales training session. Part of this session — a fairly expensive part — was to be a somewhat whimsical video that involved some sophisticated post-production efforts to create visual effects. As the video evolved from media treatment to finished script, we all began to see it in our minds' eyes and imagine it completed. We were really looking forward to experiencing the finished product.

Unfortunately, our team's enthusiastic creativity had added a few visual effects to this video that threatened to put us way over our budget. It looked like we would either have to abandon our visual effects or ask the client for more money to pay for them. Fortunately, before we had to make this tough choice, our ever-resourceful video producer came up with a creative solution: Instead of doing the post-production in the Los Angeles area, where our project was underway, we would go to Seattle, WA, where exactly the same visual effects could be produced without paying the LA studios' high prices. Even when our travel expenses were included, we would still be able to get everything we needed and not go over budget. It sounded like a perfect solution.

There was only one catch: We would be working in the Seattle studio during the lower-cost "graveyard" shift – from 11 at night to 7 in the morning. Some of the team, myself included, thought this was an awful idea. Who could think straight and make good editing decisions in the middle of the night? And what were we supposed to do in our "off" hours during the day? Again, our resourceful producer had the answer: We'd go to a horse-racing track he enjoyed. Well, from my perspective, this sounded like another awful idea (I don't gamble and I don't know anything about horse-racing). But I really wanted to get our video done and keep all of our hoped-for special effects, so I grudgingly agreed to the plan and kept my brooding and complaining to myself.

As it turned out, the entire trip was a great success. The night shift at the post-production house allowed us full access to sophisticated equipment and processes that would never have been available to us in the normal business hours. And our trips to the racetrack were a truly pleasant surprise. It was a beautiful place, set among the deep green pines with migrating geese in the infield. And it turned out to be fun people watching and learning about horse racing!

My initial attitude of begrudgingly accepting this whole experience as a necessary inconvenience and a burden cast a bit of a dark shadow over our work. However, after I discovered the positive reality of our situation and I made a dramatic shift in my attitude from grumpy-negative to enthusiastic-positive, things went really well. My dreaded, burdensome, night-shift video production became interesting, professionally-fulfilling, and even fun! With my new attitude, the whole experience was more positive and meaningful. I only regret that I hadn't chosen this attitude from the very beginning! Had I done so, I'd have been able to see the whole trip through this positive lens and the whole team could have shared in this good energy much earlier.

And here's a footnote: The result of all this was a video that not only delighted our client, but worked well as part of the sales training and ultimately won many awards from various professional film producer groups for its unique production techniques. As an added bonus, our project team had become closer by sharing some interesting travel adventures.

Overall, **the most important lesson I learned from this experience was this: I have the power — and as project manager, maybe even the obligation — to find and choose an attitude that will make things better for myself, my client and my team.** So these days I work hard to look for, and find, the best in situations. Rather than simply allowing circumstances to choose my attitude for me, I try to wake up and become conscious of my attitude and its effect on the people around me. Then, if necessary, I change it.

You Gotta Wake Up!

In **A New Earth** **Eckhart Tolle** discusses the concept of **"awakened doing."** Tolle says:

"There are three modalities of awakened doing: acceptance, enjoyment, and enthusiasm… You need… to make sure that one of them operates when you are engaged in anything at all… From the most simple task to the most complex, if you are not in a state of either acceptance, enjoyment, or enthusiasm, look closely and you will find that you are creating suffering for yourself and others."

Think about that:
" **… if you are not in a state of either acceptance, enjoyment, or enthusiasm… you are creating suffering for yourself and others.**"

If you're working with a project team, you definitely don't want to create suffering if you can help it!

From Tolle's perspective, the very least you can do to make a bad situation better is to simply accept it, without fighting it or complaining about it or giving it drama and negative energy. Then, through this calm acceptance, you can use the energy that would otherwise be consumed fighting against your circumstances to more effectively find a way to improve the situation. What's more, you might discover some enjoyment in the situation, as I did in my Seattle trip. And finally, from this place of enjoyment, you might even develop a genuine enthusiasm for what's happening. So in the case of my Seattle editing experience, I initially went from acceptance to enjoyment. And today I look forward with enthusiasm to the time when we might make another video-editing/horse racing trip!

So… *Consciously* Choose Your Attitude

The key to all this is conscious choice. **When you find yourself faced with a difficult situation, you must be conscious of your power to pick and choose an attitude that defuses negativity and encourages positive, creative engagement.** In this way, you and your project team will be much better able to accept the situation and maybe even turn it into a victory of some sort.

So how does your team respond to challenges, disappointments and set-backs? Do they spend a lot of time and energy on anger or resentment? Do they (do you?) understand that while you can't always control what happens to you, you can always control how you respond? In other words, do you all realize that **your attitude is a choice… it's not your destiny!**

Challenges...

Reflections

Reflect on these questions:
- What's the overall mood of our project team?
- Are team members (or am I) feeling resentful, angry, victimized, or some other negative attitude?
- Can we, as a team, choose another attitude?

Team Challenges

Ask your team:
- What negative attitudes are we manifesting?
- Do these negative attitudes make it easier or harder to complete our work?
- How, specifically, might we change our negative attitudes?
- What are some positive results, positive circumstances, or positive events that we can focus on that make these negative attitudes seem petty and or even silly?

Project Manager Challenges

- Observe your project team members and listen with your heart for ways that negative attitudes might be coloring their perceptions or distorting their interactions.
- Get creative: Figure out how you can "turn around" negative attitudes by re-characterizing them in terms of a "count-your-blessings" strategy. (For example, let's say you get a flat tire on the way to an important meeting and were forced to miss it. You can stew and be angry or you can count your blessings that you are important enough to be needed in that meeting and that you have a car that will transport you places most of the time!)
- Let team members vent their anger and frustration... then help them find the good in the project. Help them find ways that the "glass is half full!"

Learn More...

- Go to PhilosophersNotes (http://www.philosophersnotes.com/) and get the *full notes and MP3s* on:
  - *Man's Search for Meaning* by Viktor Frankl
  - *Meditations* by Marcus Aurelius
  - *The Enchiridion* by Epictetus
  - *The Diamond Cutter* by Geshe Michael Roach
  - *Happy for No Reason* by Marci Shimoff
  - *A New Earth* by Eckhart Tolle

- Get the 5 ½ hour audio of **Man's Search for Meaning** by Victor Frankl from **Learn Out Loud.com** -- http://www.learnoutloud.com/Product/M006050/81719

- Get the 6 hr unabridged audio of **Meditations** by Marcus Aurelius from **LearnOutLoud.com** -- http://www.learnoutloud.com/Product/T002300/81719

- Get the **_6 hour audio of Happy for No Reason_** narrated by the author herself, Marci Shimoff from **LearnOutLoud.com** -- http://www.learnoutloud.com/Product/H029015/81719

- Get the 9 1/4 hour audio of A New Earth narrated by the author himself, Eckhart Tolle from **LearnOutLoud.com** -- http://www.learnoutloud.com/Product/A016476/81719

- For related books and Kindle downloads from Amazon.com, go to the *Inspired Project Teams* blog post **"Consciously Choose Your Attitude"** and scroll to the end of the blog post. Direct links to related Amazon products are posted there: http://www.inspiredprojectteams.com/?p=1026

Be the Change You Want to See

"You must be the change you want to see in the world." - **Mahatma Gandhi**

"I can't hear your words because they are drowned out by your actions" – **Ralph Waldo Emerson**

"If you would convince a man that he does wrong, do right. Men will believe what they see." – **Henry David Thoreau**

"… if you want joy, give joy to others; if you want love, learn to give love; if you want attention and appreciation, learn to give attention and appreciation; if you want material affluence, help others to become materially affluent." -- **Deepak Chopra** in *The Seven Spiritual Laws of Success*

All these quotes point to the same powerful truth that has become an aphorism: Actions speak louder than words. What's more, implied in all these bits of wisdom is the deeper truth that when you take a heartfelt action, especially one that is rooted in giving of yourself, you somehow release into the world the same sort of energy that propelled you to take this action. The result: Other people resonate to your energy and begin to replicate your behavior. By being (or manifesting) the change you wish to see, you are actually releasing forces that conspire to bring about more of this change in the world.

OK. That sounds a little cosmic, right? Well, here are a couple of examples that will make this all a bit more real.

Picking Up the Litter

Here in the Los Angeles area, I take a daily cardio walk/run carrying weights. I walk along a groomed, palm-tree-lined city trail, complete with benches and garbage cans placed at strategic locations. A couple of months ago, I began noticing Styrofoam drinking cups and bags from chips scattered around messing up the otherwise green and well-groomed view. After I got over being irritated, I decided to see how much longer my exercises would take if I were to simply pick this stuff up and deposit it at the nearest garbage can. In all, there are usually just 4 or 5 locations where I need to stop for litter. The impact on my walk, I learned by timing it, was to add less than 60 seconds to the overall duration. That's not much impact, when weighed against the benefits of removing the visual blight.

Now along this route there's a particular bench where all the day laborers hang out, waiting for someone to come and take them to a job site for work. These guys have been the worst for littering, with all kinds of cups and bags dribbled around their bench. Now I certainly don't want to tangle with them… they are all younger and stronger than I am. Worse, I don't speak Spanish and they don't speak English, so I could barely get past a quick Hello, even if I wanted to complain. In any case, I decided to go ahead and pick up the litter around them, smiling all the while, then deposit it unceremoniously in the trash can beside their bench, and wave good-bye. Now, the first few times I did this, they looked puzzled, but tolerated me. After a few days of repeating this behavior, I started to be received with smiles and hellos. And finally, just about a week ago, I saw that they had begun to pick up the litter when they caught sight of me coming. They laughed when I got there and said, "See… It's okay… We got it!"

In fact, for the last several days, their bench area has been either trash-free or they begin picking it up when they see me coming. It's kind of good-natured game! But more importantly, the change I wanted to see (i.e., everyone picking up trash to keep the path clean) has now been manifested because I first became that change! No lectures, no complaining, no yelling… I just became the change and set loose the energy for it to manifest beyond me! How cool is that!

The Subject Matter Experts

Here's a project management example. I was once managing a large project whose goal was to create a comprehensive collection of printed and mediated training materials to support a new family of high tech products. My team of instructional designers and writers had to interview dozens of subject matter experts (SMEs) and take away technical documentation from each of these meetings to serve as references so they could simplify this stuff and turn it into training for end-users and sales people. The trouble is that most of these SMEs would show up at our meetings with copies of their overview presentations only, but no extra copies of their detailed technical documents. Without the deep detail references, my writers had nothing to work with! So, to fix this, I began asking these SMEs for their one and only single copy of these detailed documents at the beginning of each meeting, then I'd run out to the client's copying center and make copies for each of our writers while the SME and writers went ahead with their overview meeting.

As the two-week-long series of interviews progressed, I began to be greeted by SMEs who would look around for me, smile, and direct my attention to a stack of copies they had brought with them. It seems the word had spread that if they didn't bring copies, I'd be taking their documents away to make my own! So the change I wanted to see (all my writers having detailed reference documentation) had been manifested not because I complained or nagged, but because I simply "became the change" by doing the copying myself. (And yes, by the way, we had asked them to make copies in advance memos we had sent, but heck, who reads memos?!)

Project Teams Can Change!

Project teams often develop their own subcultures made up of attitudes and behaviors that aren't always positive. For example, a team might develop a habit of endlessly complaining about lack of management support or not having enough resources to do the work. Or teams might develop an overly competitive, workaholic tendency to labor into the nights and weekends at the expense of their family and personal lives.

To change these behaviors or attitudes, the project manager (or a respected team leader) must take the initiative to "be the change," modeling it and showing it to be a worthwhile adaptation. So, in the case of the endlessly complaining team, someone must stop the cycle by simply countering the complaints with an opposing point of view, citing evidence to the contrary or, better still, making it a practice to overtly state why it's fun, challenging, and career-stretching to work on the project. Or, in the case of our workaholic team, a respected team member could "be the change" and simply start going home at a more reasonable time, refusing to work weekends, and occasionally sharing some of the good things that are happening at home with family and recreation.

The key: To make changes, someone must, well… change! Someone must bravely manifest the desired behavior or attitude so it can eventually spread to the rest of the team.

Challenges…

Reflections

Reflect on these questions:
- What changes in behavior or attitude would you like to see in your organization?
- What are some potential situations that would allow you to model one of these new, changed behaviors or attitudes?
- What's stopping you from making the change? … from modeling the new behavior or attitude?

Team Challenges

Ask your team:
- What are some behaviors or attitudes you've been thinking "really ought to be changed around here." What do we need to do differently?
- Have you tried making a small, individual change in your behavior or attitude that could prove the value of this change?
- What are some of the obstacles you face when you try to implement an individual change in behavior or attitude? … How might these obstacles be removed?
- Does it make sense to ask for senior management help in removing obstacles to change?

Project Manager Challenges

- Think about your project team's stresses, irritations, or discomforts.
- Could some of these stresses, irritations, or discomforts be removed by changes in the project work flow or work process? If so, what's stopping you from supporting these changes?
- If necessary, have a serious talk with appropriate senior managers to share ways they might support important changes your project team wants to make in attitude or behavior.
- Just do it! Become (manifest by yourself) the change that would be good for your team. Be their model.
- Support and (if appropriate) praise all those little attempts your project team makes to bring about positive changes in attitude or behavior.

Learn More….

- Go to **PhilosophersNotes** (http://www.philosophersnotes.com/) and get the full **notes & MP3s** on these books:
  - Deepak Chopra's The Seven Spiritual Laws of Success
  - The Selected Writings of Ralph Waldo Emerson

- Get the 1 hr & 27 min audio of ***The Seven Spiritual Laws of Success*** narrated by the author, **Deepak Chopra**, from **LearnOutLoud.com** -- http://www.learnoutloud.com/Product/T003633/81719

- Get the ***Essential Emerson CD***, narrated by Archibald Macleish, from **LearnOutLoud.com.** -- http://www.learnoutloud.com/Product/E028499/81719

- For related books and Kindle downloads from Amazon.com, go to the *Inspired Project Teams* blog post **"Be the Change You Want to See"** and scroll to the end of the blog post. Direct links to related Amazon products are posted there: http://www.inspiredprojectteams.com/?p=806

Taking Care of Yourself:
Managing Your Priorities, Time, & Energy

In this part of the book, we provide a broad survey of some of my favorite "best practices" that can help you take charge of your priorities, better manage your time, and maintain your energy. After all, project management (even Minimalist PM) can be difficult and stressful. So why not do everything you can to maintain your edge?

This Part is divided into four main sections. Each section describes specific "best practices" which you can use to help you better manage your priorities, time and energy. The best practices discussed here include:

- **Back to Basics: Manage Your Energy**
    - Get enough sleep, rest, and water.
    - Develop "positive rituals" that run on "auto pilot."

- **Leverage Your Signature Strengths**
    - Identify your signature strengths and use them whenever you can.

- **Manage Your Time**
    - Prioritize and just say "No!"
    - Understand & deal with procrastination.
    - Avoid "multi-tasking" – It's not effective.
    - Practice "single-mindedly one touching."
    - Do what you need to do to get into "flow."
    - Control your "office hours."

- **Understand and Manage Your Stress**
    - Meditate & *reduce* your tolerance to stress.
    - Trust your judgment.
    - Feel your power to choose.
    - Develop an optimistic explanatory style.
    - Consciously choose your attitude.

Back to Basics: Manage Your Energy

Here are two of my favorite energy management best practices.

Best Practice: Get enough sleep, rest, & water.

Everybody knows you need to do these things, right? But here are some reminders why they're so important.

"All nighters" generally don't work. How many times have you heard about someone studying all night for an important test, only to show up at school, "go blank," and then blow the test? The two pictures below show why that happens.

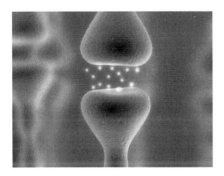 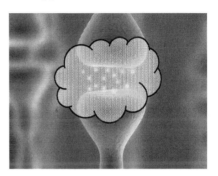

The image on the left represents a properly firing neuron in the brain, complete with an efficient electro-chemical exchange that permits good thinking. The picture on the right represents a neuron that's clogged by accumulated waste products. This neuron is unable to work properly. It's owner may think of himself as a hero-workaholic, sitting for hours and hours on end at his computer. But his brain is full of waste products and there's no way he's really thinking clearly. So he's not doing anyone any favors by working too long without rest.

These waste products can only be cleared by two things: 1) Rest… allowing blood flow to take away all the crud and bring in fresh chemicals for proper firing, and 2) nutrients that provide those fresh chemicals. The moral of the story: You gotta get enough rest and allow your brain to clear/replenish its chemicals if you want to be effective.

But don't take my word for it. Here are some quotes by a couple of guys who've spent their careers researching the topic of peak performance among athletes, business people, and others:

"… our capacity to be fully engaged depends on our ability to periodically disengage."

"[Periodization is] maximizing performance by alternating periods of activity with periods of rest… 'work-rest' ratios lie at the heart of periodization, a training method used by elite athletes throughout the world."
-- *Jim Loehr & Tony Schwartz, in* **The Power of Full Engagement**

Then there's this from Evan Robinson's review of research on working in "crunch mode:"

"Productivity starts to go down each day after 4 - 6 hours of continuous work. After enough hours, productivity goes to zero or may even become negative due to extra errors & mistakes."
-- Evan Robinson, **Why Crunch Mode Doesn't Work: 6 Lessons**
http://archives.igda.org/articles/erobinson_crunch.php

And finally, Loehr and Schwartz remind us of the value of drinking enough water:

"… research suggests that drinking at least sixty-four ounces of water at intervals throughout the day serves performance in a range of important ways.. **Inadequate hydration …. compromises concentration** and coordination."
  -- *Jim Loehr & Tony Schwartz,* **The Power of Full Engagement**

So c'mon. You know better! Make sure you get enough sleep, rest, and water.

Best Practice: Develop "positive rituals" that run on "auto pilot."

Positive rituals are activities that are good for you and that you perform regularly – almost every day. After engaging in them for a while, you just don't feel right if you skip them. In other words, they acquire their own momentum and you don't have to talk yourself into doing them. They run on "auto pilot."

"All great performers rely on positive rituals to manage their energy and regulate their behavior."
  -- *Jim Loehr & Tony Schwartz,* **The Power of Full Engagement**

Some examples of positive rituals:

- Exercise. (Remember? Blood flow to the brain, stress management, serotonin release, and a sense of well-being??)
- The practice of mindfulness, meditation, or mini-meditation.
- Sunday morning coffee on the patio
- Walking the dog in the park
- Other unique personal rituals with your family and friends.

Leverage Your Signature Strengths

Best Practice: Identify your signature strengths and use them whenever you can.

"… the highest success in living and the deepest emotional satisfaction comes from building and using your signature strengths." - *Dr. Martin Seligman in* **Authentic Happiness**

Seligman, former head of the American Psychological Association and founder of the positive psychology movement and science of happiness, has conducted substantial research on the topic of signature strengths and how they relate to happiness and success. His findings: When you identify and use your signature strengths as often as you can, particularly in your work, you will be more likely to be happy and successful.

Here are three things you can do **to leverage your signature strengths:**

- Go to Seligman's **Authentic Happiness** website (http://www.authentichappiness.org), sign up for free membership, and complete the VIA Signature Strengths Questionnaire.
- Volunteer for chores that use your Signature Strengths.
- Volunteer for projects that use your Signature Strengths.

Manage Your Time

Best Practice: Prioritize and just say "No!"

"You have to decide what your highest priorities are and have the courage --pleasantly, smilingly, nonapologetically -- to say "no" to other things. And the way you do that is by having a bigger "yes" burning inside." -- *Stephen Covey,* ***The 7 Habits of Highly Effective People***

So you need to say "No" because your bigger "Yes" is:

- Focused, high-quality results on your projects.
- A portfolio of work you can be proud of instead of a track record of failures.
- To prevent yourself from burning out.
- To have time for a richer personal life.

Specific actions you can take include:

1. Document time spent/needed on particular types of tasks in order to produce quality outcomes.
2. Document time available as compared to how you are currently spending time.
3. Create criteria for valuing each ongoing and potential assignment (e.g., supports career growth, provides exciting challenge, uses signature strengths, etc.).
4. Create a list of your ongoing and potential projects and apply the criteria to sort and prioritize them. *(The sample worksheet below shows a grid that might be used by an organization to prioritize its projects. By simply changing the rating criteria, you could use a similar approach to prioritize your projects.)*

Sample
Project Prioritization Worksheet

Project	Strategic Value	Ease	Financial Benefit	Cost	Resource Impact	Overall Priority	Notes
Project A [name]	1	3	3	5	2	2.8	
Project B [name]	5	2	4	4	4	3.8	
Project C [name]	3	5	3	3	5	3.8	
Project D [name]	2	4	3	3	5	3.4	
Project E [name]	5	3	5	3	2	3.6	
Project F [name]	1	2	2	5	4	2.4	
Project G [name]	1	2	1	2	2	1.6	

Priority ratings (your best guess or judgments) should be scored as follows:

Strategic Value? Is the project important to our overall strategies? (1 = Highly important 5 = Not important)

Ease? Will this project be fairly easy to complete? (1 = Very easy 5 = Very difficult)

Financial Benefit? Will the project's deliverables likely yield financial benefit? (1 = Highly likely 5 = Not likely)

Cost? Will this project likely cost a lot? (1 = Low cost 5 = High cost)

Resource Impact? Will this project have a great impact on our resources (people, equipment, etc.)? (1 = Low impact 5 = High impact)

Overall Priority: Average score, all five criteria.

NOTE: The *lower* the score, the *higher* the project's priority.

5. Decide how many of your high priority projects you can work on and still maintain a professional track record of quality. Then "just say no" to projects that are lower priority or simply represent more work than you can do in a high-quality fashion.

Best Practice: Understand and deal with procrastination.

"Procrastination is a mechanism for coping with the anxiety associated with starting or completing any task or decision." -- Neil Fiore in **The Now Habit**

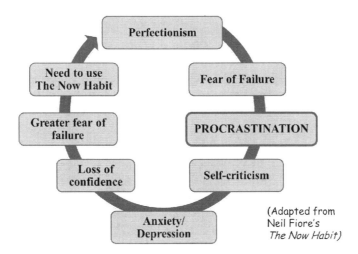

(Adapted from Neil Fiore's *The Now Habit*)

The chart above is adapted from Neil Fiore's unique description of how procrastination is part of a larger cycle of emotions, starting with perfectionism.

Here's an example of how it works. When you get that big, important project assignment, you find yourself wanting to execute it perfectly. This leads to a fear of failure that stops you in your tracks. You procrastinate. After procrastinating for a while, you begin criticizing yourself. The longer this self-criticism goes on, the greater your chances are that you'll begin to experience anxiety and depression, loss of confidence, and an even greater fear of failure! The only way you can end the cycle is to use what Fiore calls "the now habit."

Fiore recommends applying a set of **"replacement thoughts"** in order to develop "the now habit." Specifically, you need to make these replacements:

- Replace "I have to" with "I choose to."
- Replace "I must finish" with "When can I start?"
- **Replace "This project is so big and important" with "I can take one small step."**
- Replace "I must be perfect" with "I can be perfectly human."
- Replace "I don't have time to play" with "I must take time to play."

The theme here, as you can see, is to begin thinking of yourself as being empowered to take on the project on your own terms. I've highlighted the "… take one small step" replacement thought above because it is echoed by many other great thinkers as the best way to deal with fear.

As Ralph Waldo Emerson says: "Do the thing you fear and the death of fear is certain… Do the thing and you will have the power."

Then there's this from Dr. Susan Jeffers in *Feel the Fear & Do It Anyway*:

"The only way to get rid of the fear of doing something is to go out and do it... **Even if you just take a baby step or two... you need to act**... Experience a small success, overcome a little piece of your fear, and build on that." *(My bold added. -MG)*

And finally from David J. Schwartz in *The Magic of Thinking Big*:

"Here's something to remember: Actions feed and strengthen confidence; inaction in all forms feeds fear. **To fight fear, act. To increase fear — wait, put off, postpone**... Jot that down in your success rule book right now. **Action cures fear**." *(My bold added. -MG)*`

The point is that **action, in itself, is empowering.** It energizes you. You aren't frozen in place anymore, procrastinating. You are in motion, pushing through your own fear, even if it's to take a small baby step toward completing that complex project.

Finally, to remove the fear that keeps you procrastinating, **you need to trust your judgment.** I discussed this topic in quite some detail earlier in *The People Stuff* part of this book. The main thing to remember here is that you have a perfectly trustworthy "internal wisdom filter" that will generate plenty of good judgments for you if you get out of your own way and simply trust it.

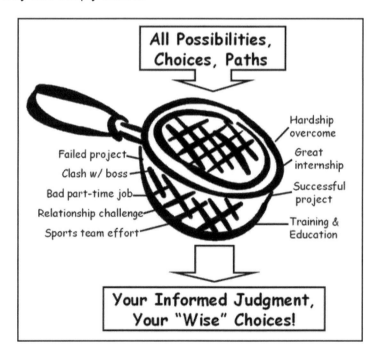

(Above: How your "internal wisdom filter" works and why you can trust your judgment! For much more on this topic, see the section above titled: "Trust Your Judgment," as well as my supporting podcast. – MG)

Summarizing, to deal with procrastination, you need to:

- Let go of perfectionism. (Be human, create something that may be flawed, and understand that most projects involve lots of polishing and revision. So it's okay if this particular iteration isn't perfect!)
- Meet fear of failure head on by taking some action, no matter how small, that moves your toward your goal.
- Recast your internal "self-talk" so that you are empowered, not victimized.
- Trust your judgment. You've earned wisdom through your experiences!

Best Practice: Avoid "multi-tasking" – It's not effective.

In a Wikipedia article titled Human Multitasking (*http://en.wikipedia.org/wiki/Human_multitasking*) psychiatrist Richard Hallowell argues that:

- Multi-tasking is a mythical activity.
- You're actually alternating rapidly between tasks.
- Errors go up and it takes longer than doing things sequentially, since time is lost as the brain continually stops, restarts, then refocuses.
- Multi-taskers are less effective & lose time in the process.

The article points out that multi-taskers frequently have the perception that they are quite effective. They believe they're getting loads of work done… and done well. However, the evidence just doesn't support these perceptions.

So if you really want to manage your time, you'd be much better off "single mindedly one touching" and doing your best to get into a "flow" state.

Best Practice: Practice "single-mindedly one touching."

"When you concentrate single-mindedly on a single task, without diversion or distraction, you get it done far faster than if you start and stop and then come back to the task and pick it up again. You can **reduce the amount of time you spend on a major task by as much as 80 percent simply by refusing to do anything else until that task is complete.**" -- Brian Tracy in *Focul Point*

I love this advice!! This practice, which I also call "single handling," is **by far my most important time management strategy.** Here's how to apply it:

1. Decide on your top priority task. (If the task will take longer than a few hours, then break it into smaller tasks that fit shorter time frames. Then pick the most important one as your top priority.)
2. Don't go online, don't check email, don't make that phone call, don't walk around and chat over coffee or do anything else. (These can wait an hour or two!)
3. Shut up and get to work! Focus on this top priority until it is done.

In their book **Rework: A Better, Easier Way to Succeed in Business**, Jason Fried & David Heinemeier Hansson warn us that to get anything done, we've got to have some quality "alone time" and break our "communications addiction." And that means you must lock yourself up and turn everything off that intrudes: No "you've got mail" announcements, no "ding-dong" bells announcing a chat message, no phone calls (Let it go to voicemail!). You might even want to hang a "do not disturb" sign on your door!

Finally, regarding email, consider this. In his **PhilosophersNote** on Tal Ben-Shahar's book **Happier**, Brian Johnson reports Ben-Shahar's findings that **checking our e-mail every few minutes takes away from our productivity and creativity** and ultimately makes us less happy. **One study shows workers so distracted suffer a greater loss of IQ than someone smoking marijuana.**

Whoa! Think about that! **If you're gonna be checking email every few minutes, you might as well be stoned!** Is that really what you want when you're trying to get your work done?! I don't think so! So break your communications addiction and let them wait a couple hours for that reply! You'll ultimately get more respect by producing high-quality results than you will from simply responding compulsively to electronic nags every 30 seconds.

Best Practice: Do what you need to do to get into "flow."

"In all the activities people in our study reported engaging in, enjoyment comes at a very specific point: whenever the opportunities for action perceived by the individual are equal to his or her capabilities." - Mihaly Csikszentmihalyi in **Flow: The Psychology of Optimal Experience**

In his great book **Flow**, Csikszentmihalyi describes how top performers in all fields are able to get themselves into a state he calls "flow." We've all experienced it. It's that feeling of being "in the zone," fully engaged and effective.

Csikszentmihalyi tells us that when a task is too difficult, it leads to anxiety and poor performance. On the other hand, when a task is too easy, it leads to boredom and doesn't keep us fully engaged. **Flow is that state of balance in which a task is just challenging enough to be engaging, without being overwhelming or frustrating.**

To get into your "flow" state:

- **Take that difficult task and break it into smaller, more doable pieces.** Then try to relax and work on these pieces slowly, one-at-a-time. If appropriate, be humble and simply ask for some help or coaching for the really tough parts. Consider it a learning experience!
- **Take that too-easy, tedious, or boring task and challenge yourself** to do it faster or combine several simpler chores into a single, more complex and challenging chore.

Best Practice: Control your "office hours."

"Interruption is the enemy of productivity…Those taps on the shoulder and little impromptu get-togethers may seem harmless, but they're actually corrosive to productivity. **Interruption is not collaboration, it's just interruption.** [These] break your work day into a series of 'work moments.'" -- Jason Fried & David Heinemeier Hansson in *Rework: A Better, Easier Way to Succeed in Business*

I once worked in a consulting firm that fought against interruptions by applying this **procedure for entering another person's office or workspace:**

- Knock on the door or cubicle wall and then wait, saying nothing.
- Wait for the person you are visiting to either 1) speak to you and welcome you in, or 2) silently hold up a hand as if saying "Stop," indicating that she is busy.
- If you're welcomed in, then you go ahead and speak, continuing your visit.
- If you get the "Stop" signal, then you simply go away without saying a word. The person who gave you this signal is duty-bound to seek you out later, when she is finished with her chore.

Now this may sound overly formal, but it worked great! We were all much more productive (and less irritable from random interruptions) than before this policy was implemented. You might try it in your office.

Here are some other ways you might control your office hours:

- **Set interrupt-free hours versus collaboration hours.** For example, establish a policy of no meetings from 8 a.m. to 10 a.m. or 2 p.m. to 4 p.m. every day.
- **Establish "quiet zones" versus interaction zones.** For example, you might decide that all individual offices are quiet zones or that a certain cluster of cubicles is a quiet zone. Then designate a specific conference room or office as the place for conversations.
- **Work at home in your "alone zone."** Sometimes it's simply better to work at home, without distractions. You might set up one or two days a week for this and make it a regular productivity-enhancing practice. (Here's a bit of related trivia: Most independent consultants I know report that they typically can get 8 hours of "at the office" work done in a mere 5 hours when they work at home, alone and uninterrupted.)

Understand and Manage Your Stress

Best Practice: Meditate & *reduce* your tolerance to stress.

I'm a huge believer in the power of meditation. I start every day with a 20 minute meditation. Now I'm not talking about any particular religious practice, but the secular practice of mindful meditation. The purpose isn't to achieve some blissed-out cosmic state, but to bring your full awareness into the present moment. And that means you make better decisions.

I got my introduction to mindful meditation through the works of **Jon Kabat-Zinn,** Professor of Medicine Emeritus and founding director of the Stress Reduction Clinic and the Center for Mindfulness in Medicine, Health Care, and Society at the University of Massachusetts Medical School. Kabat-Zinn started his career as **a scientist at MIT** and it is with this scientific perspective (along with his clinical research to support many of his positions) that he shares his thoughts on the power of mindfulness. He teaches **mindfulness meditation as a technique to help people cope with stress, anxiety, pain and illness.** In his words, **mindfulness (achieved through mindful meditation) is "paying attention, on purpose, to the present moment, without judgment."**

So why practice mindfulness? What's in it for you, as a project manager or creative project team member? Better decisions. Clearer distinctions and analyses. More powerful judgments. Less stress. What's in it for you, as a spouse, parent, or friend? The ability to participate in relationships more fully, more compassionately, and more authentically.

Here are some other benefits of mindfulness and mindful meditation:

- Greater awareness of jabbering background voices in your head (worrying, self-criticizing, etc.)
- Ability to dismiss these voices with a "light touch"
- Reduced willingness to tolerate these voices (and the ability to "let them go")
- Reduced willingness to tolerate feelings of stress (and the ability to just let these stressful feelings go)
- Greater clarity, "brighter" awareness of "now"
- Greater ability to concentrate, be creative
- Many physical health benefits (Mindfulness is often prescribed by physicians, and paid for by health care insurance, to treat stress and stress-related illness.)

For lots more information, as well as links to podcasts, videos, and free audio guided meditation tools, see my blog post and podcast **Practice Mindfulness** http://www.inspiredprojectteams.com/?p=766

Best Practice: Trust your judgment.

"Every time you don't follow your inner guidance, you feel a loss of energy, loss of power, a sense of spiritual deadness." – Shakti Gawain

One of the most self-defeating things you can do is drive yourself crazy second-guessing yourself. This can be incredibly stressful! The cure for this is to trust your judgment. As I showed you a few pages ago, you have an "inner wisdom filter" that can be trusted. You already know what you need to know!

So this best practice is simple: Look at that internal wisdom filter of yours – all those experiences and challenges you've overcome – and know that you have what it takes to make good judgments. Then stop doubting yourself.

Try this simple exercise: Are you facing a difficult decision in which you're afraid your judgment can't be trusted? Then make a list of the following:

- Specific skills you have that relate to this decision
- Specific experiences in this area in which you have successfully prevailed and succeeded
- Specific times you have faced an "unknown," then rallied and prevailed

Now look at your list. Do you see why you should relax and trust your judgment?

Best Practice: Feel your power to choose.

"Understand that the right to choose your own path is a sacred privilege. Use it. Dwell in possibility." -- Oprah Winfrey

It's stressful being a victim. It's stressful to feel that your fate is in someone else's hands and that you have no power over what happens to you. But in most cases this feeling is simply not real. In most cases you have the power to make all sorts of choices. You simply need to realize this power to choose.

You can prove this to yourself by revisiting Neil Fiore's **"replacement thoughts"** (from **The Now Habit**) discussed earlier. Specifically, think about how you can assert your power to make choices for yourself as you try to make these mental replacements:

- Replace "I have to" with "I choose to."
- Replace "I must finish" with "When can I start?"
- Replace "This project is so big and important" with "I can take one small step."
- Replace "I must be perfect" with "I can be perfectly human."
- Replace "I don't have time to play" with "I must take time to play."
- (Ask yourself: What other "I'm a victim" thoughts might I be able to replace with "Hey, I choose to do this…" thoughts? Then make the replacement!)

When you work through this process of replacing your "victim" thoughts with thoughts that reflect your power to choose, you soon begin to feel your strength and reduce your stress.

Best Practice: Develop an optimistic explanatory style.

One of the most stressful things people can do to themselves is to process and reprocess events in negative terms – to talk to themselves in an ongoing pessimistic monologue that continually asserts that life is bad and they themselves are the reason that everything is going wrong. It's extremely stressful to live within this self-imposed gray cloud. Worse yet, as Martin Seligman's research has shown, living like this is entirely unnecessary. You have the power to change the way you explain the world to yourself – **you have the power to change your explanatory style.**

"One of the most significant findings in psychology in the last twenty years is that individuals can choose the way they think…. On a mechanical level, **cognitive therapy works because it changes explanatory style from pessimistic to optimistic, and the change is permanent.** It gives you a set of cognitive skills for talking to yourself when you fail." -- Dr. Martin Seligman in **Learned Optimism: How to Change Your Mind & Your Life.**

In conducting the research that led him to these conclusions, Seligman observed many professional sports teams, as well as management teams in large corporations. In particular, he compared how these teams dealt with failure and how they talked to themselves after a setback. Here are a few of his conclusions:

- Optimistic people (optimistic explanatory style) can "bounce back" from a loss more quickly, learn from their mistakes, and get better results the next time.
- Pessimistic people can't recover as quickly.
- "Unlike dieting, learned optimism is easy to maintain once you start. Once you get into the habit of disputing negative beliefs, your daily life will run much better, and you will feel much happier." -- Seligman in **Learned Optimism: How to Change Your Mind & Your Life**

As many other researchers have reported, the human brain is fairly plastic – you can "rewire" it by simply using it repeatedly in a new way. And, according to Seligman and his researchers, you can change your way of thinking from pessimistic to optimistic by changing your "explanatory style."

In a nutshell, there are **three dimensions of explanatory style**: permanence, pervasiveness, and personalization. When you "talk to yourself" after a victory or after a defeat, you classify the experience according to these dimensions. You ask yourself these questions:
- *Permanence*: Is it permanent? (Will it continue?)
- *Pervasiveness*: Is it universal? (Does it affect everything I do?)
- *Personalization*: Is it "my fault?" (Did I cause or create this situation?)

Here are a couple of examples to illustrate how an optimistic team, as compared to a pessimistic team, might use their unique explanatory styles to handle good news and bad news.

Example: "Good news! They loved our design!"

The Pessimist Says:
- "We got lucky." (It's <u>not permanent</u>.)
- "They never like our stuff." (It's <u>not pervasive</u>.)
- "They're easing up on their evaluation criteria." (It's <u>not personal.</u> It's nothing we did.)

The Optimist Says:
- "It figures! We do great work!" (It's <u>permanent</u>.)
- "Look at all these other projects that went well." (It's <u>pervasive</u>.)
- "We worked hard on this, applied a bunch of great strategies." (It's <u>personal</u>.)

In the example above, each team got the same good news: the client loved their design. The pessimistic team, however, shrugs off the good news as no big deal... almost as though it's an accident. In contrast, the optimistic team embraces the good news as though they earned it and will always earn such news. In other words, the optimists process good news as something they deserve – it strengthens their team and increases their confidence and the likelihood of success on future projects. The pessimists miss the opportunity to "own" the good news and grow stronger from it. In fact, they distance themselves from the good news, decreasing their chances of developing a pattern of success.

Example: "Bad news! They hated our design!"

The Pessimist Says:
- "It figures! We can't seem to win!" (It's <u>permanent</u>.)
- "We've had 3 other losing designs this year!" (It's <u>pervasive</u>.)
- "We're just not creative enough!" (It's <u>personal</u>.)

The Optimist Says:
- "This is a fluke. Clients usually like our stuff! " (It's not <u>permanent</u>.)
- "We've had 2 other winning designs this year!" (It's <u>not pervasive.</u>)
- "They missed telling us a couple of key things & we'll get it right next time." (It's <u>not personal.</u>)

In the case of bad news (above), the teams switch roles. The pessimists readily "own" this bad news and predict that they will likely get more of it in the future. In contrast, the optimists shrug off the bad news as a fluke. In fact, they go so far as to cite specific reasons why the bad news is simply a one-time event. The result: the optimistic team has "circled their wagons" mentally and not allowed the bad news to damage their chances of winning in the next project.

So how about you? Are you ready to rewire your brain so that your explanatory style is consistently optimistic? If so, you are likely to reduce your stress and increase your chances of success.

Specifically, here's **how you can develop an optimistic explanatory style:**

- *When you get bad news*, talk to yourself and provide yourself with evidence that the bad news is 1) not permanent... it won't last forever, 2) not pervasive... there are lots of other areas where you are getting contrasting good news, and 3) it's not personal... it's not completely your fault.

- *When you get good news*, talk to yourself and provide yourself with evidence that the good news is 1) permanent... likely to continue coming, 2) pervasive... happening in many other areas of your work or life, and 3) personal... you deserve it and it results from your hard work, talent, experience, etc.

By practicing these optimistic responses to good and bad news, you'll develop your own "learned optimism," eventually rewiring your brain to automatically respond optimistically. And this will not only reduce stress by taking you out of that dark cloud of negative self-talk, it will increase your confidence and your chances of success in everything you do.

Best Practice: Consciously choose your attitude.

"We cannot choose our external circumstances, but we can always choose how we respond to them." -- Epictetus in **The Enchiridion**

"From the most simple task to the most complex, **if you are not in a state of either acceptance, enjoyment, or enthusiasm, look closely and you will find that you are creating suffering for yourself and others.**" -- Eckhart Tolle in **A New Earth**

Take another look at the Tolle quote above. The selection in bold tells the whole story. The graphic below illustrates how one man's thrashing against reality – his self-chosen misery – is creating suffering for himself and others!

So what should this guy be doing? Well, according to Tolle, **he only has three choices.**

1. He can **accept his situation** and stop wasting energy fighting against it. (This will allow him to think more clearly and figure out how to make things better.)
2. He can find something to **enjoy** about the situation.
3. He can become **enthusiastic** about the situation.

Any of these choices will make things better for himself and those around him.

Now when you think about it, he actually has a fourth choice: He can remove himself from the situation by simply quitting his job. That is, he can go somewhere else and do something else that won't make him so unhappy. But if he can't quit or remove himself, then he must accept, enjoy, or become enthusiastic about his situation. To thrash around against reality, bemoaning the situation and spilling negative energy all over other people, is simply stupid. Worse, it saps away energy that could be used to make the changes that could improve things.

So the next time you find yourself ranting and raving and thrashing around against reality, refer to the chart below. See if you can't reduce your stress and make things better for everyone around you by consciously choosing a different attitude!

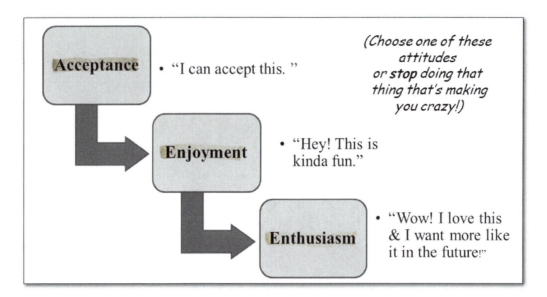

For more about how you can "Consciously Choose Your Attitude," see the 3rd part of this book (above): *The People Stuff: 10 Sets of Challenges to Inspire Teams*. And you can also check out my 18-minute podcast, *Consciously Choose Your Attitude*. Download it from – http://www.inspiredprojectteams.com/?p=1026

Summary

In this Part of the book I've provided a very quick overview of some powerful "best practices" that can help you take better care of the resource that is you! Specifically, I challenged you to apply these best practices to manage your priorities, time, & energy.

- **Back to Basics: Manage Your Energy**
  - Get enough sleep, rest, and water.
  - Develop "positive rituals" that run on "auto pilot."

- **Leverage Your Signature Strengths**
  - Identify your signature strengths and use them whenever you can.

- **Manage Your Time**
  - Prioritize and just say "No!"
  - Understand & deal with procrastination.
  - Avoid "multi-tasking" – It's not effective.
  - Practice "single-mindedly one touching."
  - Do what you need to do to get into "flow."
  - Control your "office hours."

- **Understand and Manage Your Stress**
  - Meditate & *reduce* your tolerance to stress.
  - Trust your judgment.
  - Feel your power to choose.
  - Develop an optimistic explanatory style.
  - Consciously choose your attitude.

Learn More

The information above is just the tip of the iceberg! If you resonate to some of these best practices, you really ought to go to the original source and do some further reading to deepen your understanding. Many of the books have exercises, checklists, and other tools that can help you put these ideas to work immediately in your life. To learn more check out one of these resources:

- A Philosopher's Notes - On Optimal Living, Creating an Authentically Awesome Life and Other Such Goodness *by Brian Johnson* **[!!! Start here!!! This is good stuff! - MG]**
- The Power of Full Engagement: Managing Energy, Not Time, Is the Key to High Performance and Personal Renewal *by Jim Loehr & Tony Schwartz*
- "Why Crunch Mode Doesn't Work: 6 Lessons" *(online article) by Evan Robinson* http://archives.igda.org/articles/erobinson_crunch.php
- Authentic Happiness: Using the New Positive Psychology to Realize Your Potential for Lasting Fulfillment *by Martin E. P. Seligman*
- The 7 Habits of Highly Effective People *by Stephen R. Covey*
- "What's Project Portfolio Management (PPM) and Why Should Project Managers Care About It?" – *online article by Michael Greer* http://michaelgreer.biz/?p=147
- "Too Many Projects? Prioritize Them!" – *online article by Michael Greer* http://michaelgreer.biz/?p=138
- The Now Habit: A Strategic Program for Overcoming Procrastination and Enjoying Guilt-Free Play by Neil A. Fiore
- Feel the Fear & Do It Anyway *by Dr. Susan J. Jeffers*
- The Magic of Thinking Big *by David J. Schwartz*
- "Trust Your Judgment" *(Inspired Project Teams podcast by Michael Greer)* http://www.inspiredprojectteams.com/?p=691
- "Human Multitasking" *(Wikipedia article)* featuring psychiatrist Richard Hallowell http://en.wikipedia.org/wiki/Human_multitasking
- Focal Point: A Proven System to Simplify Your Life, Double Your Productivity, and Achieve All Your Goals *by Brian Tracy*
- Rework: A Better, Easier Way to Succeed in Business *by Jason Fried & David Heinemeier Hansson*
- Happier: Learn the Secrets to Daily Joy and Lasting Fulfillment *by Tal Ben-Shahar's*
- Flow: The Psychology of Optimal Experience *by Mihaly Csikszentmihalyi*
- "Practice Mindfulness" *(Inspired Project Teams podcast by Michael Greer)* http://www.inspiredprojectteams.com/?p=766
- Coming to Our Senses: Healing Ourselves and the World Through Mindfulness by *Jon Kabat-Zinn*
- The Mindfulness Revolution: Leading Psychologists, Scientists, Artists, and Meditation Teachers on the Power of Mindfulness in Daily Life (A Shambhala Sun Book) *by Barry Boyce, Jon Kabat-Zinn, Daniel Siegel, and Thich Nhat Hanh*
- Learned Optimism: How to Change Your Mind & Your Life *by Dr. Martin Seligman*
- A New Earth: Awakening to Your Life's Purpose *by Eckhart Tolle*

* Glossary of Terms Used

Throughout this text you will sometimes see a term with an asterisk (*) beside it. Below are the full, official (and sometimes a bit puffed up!) definitions of these terms. (Most are from *The Project Manager's Partner, 2nd Edition (My textbook... This is the source of much of the content in the preceding Steps!)* -- http://michaelgreer.biz/?p=208

- **Deliverables** -- Any measurable, tangible, verifiable output that must be produced to complete the project. Deliverables take **two forms: Interim outputs** (such as video scripts, floor plans, or marketing analyses) and **final deliverables** associated with these interim outputs (such as the completed video presentation, the finished building, or a completed product marketing plan).

- **Milestones** -- A significant event in the project, usually completion of a major deliverable. Milestones differ from project to project depending on the type of deliverables the project is designed to create. In project management software, a milestone is an activity that has been assigned zero duration (usually marking the end of an activity or phase).

- **Phase** – A collection of logically related project activities, usually resulting in the completion of a major deliverable. By organizing project activities into a few major phases, it is easier to plan the project, discuss project events with team members, and analyze and track the project. The exact phases used in a project typically are established by professional standards in a particular industry. (For example, motion picture projects might include scripting and shooting phases, while construction projects might include a blueprint phase, foundation building phase, and so on. The phases reflect the "best practices" of professionals in those industries.)

- **Project** -- A temporary endeavor undertaken to create a unique product or service. Typically, a project is a one-time effort to accomplish an explicit objective by a specific time. Like the individual activities that make up the project, each project has a distinguishable start and finish and a time frame for completion.

- **Resources** -- Anything a project team needs to do its job. Resources might take the form of people, equipment, facilities, funding or anything that helps perform the work.

- **Rework** -- The correction of defective work. Rework may take place either before, during or after inspection or testing. (Unnecessary rework often happens when stakeholders are not engaged early enough, but instead are shown project deliverables too late – after much time, effort, and labor dollars have been consumed.)

- **Sponsor** -- The customer, client, final owner, or entity providing funds for the project. The sponsor also typically has the power to approve the use of other resources (such as staff members, equipment, and facilities) and/or stop the project.

- **Stakeholders** -- Individuals and organizations who are involved in, or may be affected by, project activities. Typical stakeholders include the project sponsor (the person or organization paying the bills and able to stop the project—sometimes called client, customer, or funder), suppliers, contractors, vendors, craftspeople, the project manager, government agencies, and the public.

For lots **more definitions** of any and all PM terms go to:

▲ *Wideman Comparative Glossary of Project Management Terms* --
http://www.maxwideman.com/pmglossary/index.htm

PM Minimalist Values Explained

These PM Minimalist Values may be applied to any project in any industry or professional practice. The object of each of these is to **challenge you to apply "just enough" project management (PM) discipline to your projects** to keep them running smoothly, **while challenging you to drop the PM stuff that bloats** your schedules & makes people crazy.

- Create fewer deliverables with fewer features.

    Every deliverable, every feature shoots out tendrils and roots all through your project. Every little item you leave on your wish list will chew up time and effort as your team works to define it, create it, revise it, and finalize it. So the object of the game here is to consciously set out to create a little less than you might need. That way, when the inevitable swelling of your deliverables or list of features happens, your budget and schedule aren't completely blown away. (And who knows: Starting with a lean set of deliverables and features might force the team to create a cleaner, more elegant finished product!)

- Do less work.

    In an ideal world, project deliverables would be built by experts who, working all by themselves, take exactly the right actions and expend "just enough" effort to get a great finished product. And, in this ideal world, these experts wouldn't need to sync their work with reviewers or other experts or anyone else. They'd just do what needs done and get great results. Unfortunately, most of us can't work like this. We almost always have to involve other people and use review/revise cycles to build our deliverables through a series of successive approximations. But that doesn't mean we should allow the work process to get so complex that it sucks all the joy out of the practice of our professions.

    So here's the test: Ask your experts – the people who are building your deliverables – to tell you the fewest number of steps they would use to complete their work if it were up to them, working all by themselves. Then compare your experts' minimalist list of steps to the usual list of steps your projects endure. What can you cut? How can you streamline? How can you do "just enough" work to get the job done, without making people jump through a bunch of unnecessary hoops? The object of the game: Do less work, while making sure the work you must do has real added value.

- Absorb or neutralize (but don't ignore) anyone who can reject or rethink your deliverables.

    Usually the most irritating and demoralizing challenge any project team faces is unnecessary rework – being forced to redo your deliverables because somebody has "come out of the woodwork" with their own unique specifications and perspectives and challenged what you are doing. What a waste of time!

    There are two ways to deal with this situation. You can prevent it from happening by making sure you include on your project team, right from the start, everybody who has this "reject or rethink" power. In other words, you absorb them into the team and make their thinking part of the project definition. On the other hand, if they can't or won't work on your team, there's only one thing to do: You gotta neutralize them. And you do this by getting some sort of formal approval, preferably in writing, from your sponsor or customer that it's okay to simply disregard this person's input.

Review stakeholders w/sponsor – who has power to influence project?

One thing's certain: You can't just ignore them. If you try, they will eventually (maybe after you've invested loads of hours and money in your project), start screaming and you'll be stuck with a major "do over." So deal with them the right way: Absorb them into the team or formally neutralize them with your sponsor or customer's support.

- Work as fast as quality permits – maybe faster!

Everyone wants a quality finished product. But that doesn't mean that you have to slowly and methodically polish everything before you hand it off for review or hand it over to the next team member for their enhancement. Most projects can't afford such perfectionism.

In fact, there are three reasons why perfectionism doesn't make sense for most projects. First, perfectionism is often nothing more than an idiosyncratic perspective held by one person – a different person looking at the same product might define "perfect" in a different way. Second, almost all projects that involve more than one person are iterative – the deliverables are almost always "works in progress" that are continually evolving by moving from person to person and getting tweaked in one way or another. So trying to get them perfect before you hand them off can be a waste of time. Finally, perfectionism simply takes too long and is impossible to achieve. Anything that has ever been created by any human is subject to the view held by another human that it could be improved in some way. So there is no "perfect."

The point: Your project team should forget about wasting time on perfectionism and instead work as fast as they can to get reasonably good results.

- Deliver something – anything – as soon as possible.

The object of the game here is to "smoke out" any objections or desired changes from reviewers as early as possible. This way you are less likely to invest a lot of time in building something only to have reviewers ask you to build it differently. By giving them something to look at early (no matter how raw), you get a chance to modify it early. This saves everyone time. And it saves your experts the frustration of having to make changes to something in which they've invested a lot of effort and creativity.

- "Make it real" as often as possible with models, mock-ups, prototypes, & samples.

The object of the game here is the same as in the suggestion above: to "smoke out" any objections or desired changes as early as possible. However, the emphasis here is on transforming vague or abstract specifications into tangible realities that reviewers can experience more accurately. So, for example, instead of looking at a list of written specs that require them to imagine what's coming, they get to handle a model or a prototype and come to know more deeply what you're doing. Either way the goal is the same: less rework and fewer painful changes.

- **Revise or reject something as soon as possible.**

    Are you seeing a theme here? The preceding two suggestions were designed to help your team find out about objections and desired changes ASAP. This suggestion extends that same theme: Take action quickly to revise – or reject, if necessary – any of your project's work products that aren't working right. In this way you can salvage as much of your schedule and budget as you can instead of allowing broken deliverables to suck up too much time or effort.

- **Give up on the project earlier; cut your losses.**

    You gotta know when to quit, already! If you are reworking and reworking and getting nowhere or if you are begging for resources that never appear or if you are trying to build something that just doesn't seem to want to be built… it may be time to just bag it and cut your losses. Remember: If you want people to work with you again on another project or if you want your boss or customer to trust your ability to handle another project in the future, you need to have the courage (supported by a well-documented set of reasons) to walk away when it's time.

- **Ignore external-to-the-project "professionals" who would have you puff up the project or its work processes.**

    There are at least six major, well-known PM certification bodies and many, many less obscure PM groups who would like you to do things their way. And there are countless organizations representing other professionals who may represent particular specialists on your project team. This is almost certain: If you perform all the professional "best practices" of most of these organizations, your project is likely to get more complicated and maybe even become severely bloated.

    You don't need a degree in medicine to practice CPR. And you don't need professional certification to decide for yourself what constitutes a set of "best practices" for your project team. So take charge: You and the experts on your team decide what you mean by "just enough" deliverables and "just enough" work processes. Then ignore all those external-to-the-project "professionals" and tell them to mind their own business!

- **Enjoy creating; don't put up with simply slogging through.**

    Projects are the most goal-oriented of human endeavors. And if you spend most of your life working on projects, as so many of our project team members do, you can develop an uneasy, ever-present sense that you are never really finished. There's a continual nagging feeling that you've not completed your work because the next goal is endlessly popping up in front of you, demanding your attention.

    So where's the joy in the work itself? What about the intrinsic value of your chosen profession? The beauty and fascination of the field itself? If you want people to be able to keep their edge, maintain their creativity, and continue to choose to be part of your organization's work force, you'll make sure they get some enjoyment out of their projects.

    How? That's up to you. After all, it's your organization. You need to take responsibility for shaping its work practices and culture. But **you can start by making sure you're doing "just enough" PM to enhance the work – and not so much that you smother the life out of it.**

The PM Minimalist Integration Guide: Adopting Project Management Minimalism in Your Organization

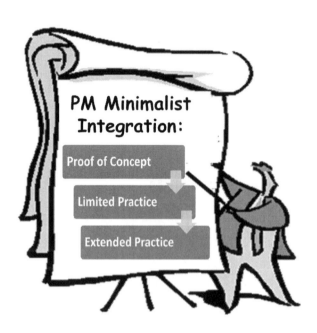

Overview

Are you ready to begin practicing Project Management Minimalism throughout your organization?

This guide provides tools to help your organization gradually integrate Project Management Minimalist practices. These tools include:

- Integration Stage 1: Proof of Concept
- Integration Stage 2: Limited Practice
- Integration Stage 3: Extended Practice

Integration Stage 1: Proof of Concept

The object of the game in Stage1: Proof of Concept is to test PM Minimalism in your organization by using the Minimalist approach to complete a single project.

(See "Resources to Support PM Minimalism Integration" at the end of this document for references that can help everyone in your organization learn more about PM Minimalism.)

Work through the following **PM activities for a single "showcase" project:**

- ❑ ***Create a Project Charter.***

    Create a Project Charter that includes all the items outlined in the "*Worksheet: The Project Charter.*"* Have this Charter reviewed & approved by your supervisor or project sponsor.
    (See Step 1: Define the project concept, then get support and approval.)*

- ❑ ***Organize the Project Team.***

    Get together everyone who'll help build the finished product, who'll use it, or who might cause trouble or force it to be changed if they don't like it. Using some of the tools from Step 2 in the Minimalist, get the team organized and hold an effective Kickoff meeting.
    (See Step 2: Get your team together and start the project.)*

- ❑ ***Build a "wish list" of deliverables. ("Go wide!")***

    Working as a team, brainstorm to create a "wide view" list of "wished for" deliverables. Pretend your team could build anything they want.
    (See Step 3: Figure out exactly what the finished work products will be.)*

- ❑ ***Reduce the "wish list" to "must build" items. (Slash & burn!)***

    Working as a team, divide the "wide view" list of deliverables into three equal-sized lists: 1) Those we "must build," 2) Those we "could build," and 3) Those we "can wait to build."
    (See Step 3: Figure out exactly what the finished work products will be.)*

- ❑ ***Describe tasks, phases and assignments.***

    Working as a team, list the tasks required to create the "must build" items. If it makes sense to do so, display them as a network diagram or other graphic so it's easy to see the phases, work flow, bottlenecks, and so on. Build in plenty of small iterations and opportunities for stakeholder review, feedback, and revision.

    Assign these tasks to specific people on your project team.
    (See Step 4: Figure out what to do…& Step 2 [Responsibility/Acct. Matrix].)*

- ❑ ***Estimate time, effort, and resources needed.***

    Still working as a team, make your best guess about how long it will take each

assigned resource to complete his or her assigned tasks. Capture your guesses in an Effort/Duration Table.
(See Step 5: Estimate time, effort, resources.*)

- ❏ **Make a project schedule:**

   Referring to a calendar, make a schedule for your project by plotting the tasks across specific dates. Include each task, specific deadlines, dates, and the names of people assigned to each task.

   Your schedule can take any form you want: Gantt chart, regular calendar, text table, etc. *(Optional:* Create sub-schedules for specific team members, for specific deliverables, specific phases, or any other logical sub-divisions of the schedule that will help your team better understand the project and their specific responsibilities.)
   (See Step 6: Build a schedule.*)

   CAUTION: *If your project schedule exceeds one month, try to break your project into a series of smaller projects. Then choose the project you want to work on first. Then continue with the activities below.*

- ❏ **Get all of the preceding planning artifacts approved.**

   Provide the project sponsor, customer, key stakeholders, and other important project players with copies of all the planning artifacts you created in the previous steps. Then ask them to approve these, in writing, as the overall plan that will guide your project team.
   (See Step 10: Close out.. "Worksheet: Project Sign-Off Form"*)

- ❏ **Get started.**

   Complete the tasks as described in your overall plan..
   (See Steps 8: Keep ... moving, 9: Handle scope changes, & 10: Close out...*)

- ❏ **Inspect and correct.**

   While the project is under way, find out:
   - Are "must build" items on time?
   - Are "must build" items of high enough quality?
   - Is everyone doing what they promised?
   - Do people need more help or need obstacles removed?
   - What must we correct or fix to finish the project on time?
   - Are we getting the formal "sign offs" we need on phases and on the finished project? If not, what do we need to do to get these formal approvals?

   (See Steps 8: Keep ... moving, 9: Handle scope changes, & 10: Close out...*)

- ❏ **Conduct a project post-mortem & report lessons learned.**

   When the project is over, look back & figure out how you could have improved it

by conducting a formal "post-mortem" review. List any Lessons Learned, then describe how you can use these to make you next project better.
(See Step 10: Close out phases, close out the project.*)

- **Debrief Integration Stage 1: Proof of Concept.**
    - Get together with senior managers and anyone who wants to improve PM in your organization, then review the post-mortem findings and lessons learned.
    - Answer these questions:
        - Could the processes used on this "showcase" project be applied to other projects with positive results? (i.e., Would these processes help us improve our current project work process or improve the quality of our deliverables?)
        - What enhancements do we need to make to our PM Minimalism practice?
        - Should we continue to Integration Stage 2: Limited Practice?
        - If yes, what are some projects that would be good candidates for testing the PM Minimalist approach?
    - *If senior managers or other PM change agents agree to do so,* **move on to Integration Stage 2: Limited Practice.**

---

* For detailed info on this Step (i.e., Results, Process, Tools/Worksheets, etc.) see
The Project Management Minimalist: Just Enough PM to Rock Your Projects!
(http://michaelgreer.biz/?page_id=636)

Integration Stage 2: Limited Practice

The purpose of Stage1: Proof of Concept was to test PM Minimalism in your organization by using the Minimalist approach on a single project. In this Stage, you expand your testing of the PM Minimalist concept to include three more projects.

Here are the activities involved:

- ***Identify at least three more projects that might be managed using a Minimalist approach.***

- ***For each project, complete all "Stage 1: Proof of Concept" activities*** that were used in the single-project Proof of Concept test. (If your management group decided to modify these in some way, then ask each team to use the newly modified process.)

- ***Debrief Integration Stage 2: Limited Practice.***
    - Get together with senior managers and anyone who wants to improve PM in your organization, then review the post-mortem findings and lessons learned for each of the three projects involved in this "Limited Practice" integration stage. (Include those who attended the debriefing of Stage 1: Proof of Concept, but don't limit the discussion to these people only. Include anyone from the three Integration Stage 2 project teams who would like to participate.)
    - Answer these questions:
        - Could the processes used on these "limited practice" projects be applied to still more projects with positive results? (i.e., improved work process or improved quality of deliverables?)
        - What enhancements do we need to make to our PM Minimalism practice?
        - Should we continue to Integration Stage 3: Extended Practice?
    - *If senior managers or other PM change agents agree to do so,* ***move on to Integration Stage 3: Extended Practice.***

Integration Stage 3: Extended Practice

The purpose of Stage1: Proof of Concept and Stage 2: Limited Practice was to test PM Minimalism in your organization by using the Minimalist approach on a limited number of projects. In this Stage, you will be extending the PM Minimalist concept to all new projects for the period of one year.

Here are the activities involved:

- Select a core team of volunteers to serve as PM Minimalist mentors. (These should be people who worked with the Stages 1 & 2 Integration efforts.)

- Based on what you learned from Integration Stages 1 & 2, create a list of "Recommended PM Activities" to be undertaken by all projects that will be starting within the next year. You might also create a list of "Potential Pitfalls to Avoid."

- Assemble any documentation, local rules of thumb or estimating guidelines, copies of **The Project Management Minimalist**, or any other references that can help project managers apply PM Minimalism. (Refer to the "Learn More" section at the end of this document for additional resources, including videos and a podcast.)

- Conduct a PM Minimalism Kickoff session in which you orient project managers to the PM Minimalist processes, values, special adaptations, etc.

- **For all projects undertaken in the next year, complete all "Stage 1: Proof of Concept" activities** that were used in the single-project Proof of Concept test. If your PM integration team has decided to modify these in some way, then ask each project team to use the newly modified process.

    NOTE: Be sure that all project teams conduct post-mortem reviews and create Lessons Learned summaries.

[Time passes...] After about a year of Stage 3: Extended Practice, do the following:

- **Debrief Integration Stage 3: Extended Practice.**

    - Conduct a "whole organization" debriefing and brainstorming session.

    - Review highlights from the post-mortem findings and lessons learned for projects involved in this "Extended Practice" integration stage.

    - Answer these questions:
        - Could the processes used on these "extended practice" projects be applied to still more projects with positive results? (i.e., improved work process or improved quality of deliverables?)
        - What enhancements do we need to make to our PM Minimalism practice?
        - Should we continue to with our practice of PM Minimalism?

    - If senior managers and other PM change agents agree to do so, formalize the practice of PM Minimalism in your organization.

    - *(Optional)* **Revisit** your organization's PM Minimalism practice **every year** and work through the debriefing and brainstorming steps above to improve and refine your PM Minimalist practices.

Resources to Support PM Minimalist Integration

Want to adopt *PM Minimalism* throughout your organization? Here are some online tools you can share with other people in your organization to get the ball rolling.
(All except *The Project Management Minimalist* e-book are free.)

- ☑ **The PM Minimalist Integration Guide: Adopting Project Management Minimalism in Your Organization**
  http://michaelgreer.biz/PM-Minimalist-Integration-Guide-Ver-1.pdf
  (This is an online, stand-alone version of the document you are now reading.)

- ☑ **The PM Minimalist Quick Start Guide: The Absolute Least You Can Do!**
  (***http://michaelgreer.biz/PM-Minimalist-Quick-Start-Guide-Ver-1.pdf***)
  Includes:
  - ➢ Project Management Minimalist Quick Start Checklist
  - ➢ PM Minimalist Values Checklist
  - ➢ PM Minimalist Values Explained

- ☑ **10 Steps to Project Success (from The Project Management Minimalist)**
  (free 1-page PDF download) http://michaelgreer.biz/10steps.pdf

- ☑ **The Project Management Minimalist: Just Enough PM to Rock Your Projects!** *[The e-book]* http://michaelgreer.biz/?page_id=636

- ☑ **Free Video Series: Become a Project Management Minimalist**
  http://michaelgreer.biz/?p=930

- ☑ **Become a Project Management Minimalist** *(free 37-minute podcast & blog post w/team Challenges)* http://www.inspiredprojectteams.com/?p=1272

- ☑ **PM Minimalist Selected by Laureate Education for use in Walden University**
  http://michaelgreer.biz/?p=1078

- ☑ **Do-It-Yourself PM Certification: How to Document Your Skills & Get the Credibility You've Earned without Jumping Through Someone Else's Hoops** -- http://michaelgreer.biz/Do-It-Yourself-PM-Certification.pdf

- ☑ **Michael Greer's Customized, On-Site PM Workshops --**
  http://michaelgreer.biz/?page_id=55

  Would you like to conduct a facilitated workshop to give people a direct experience with PM Minimalism and a chance to discuss it in a "safe" classroom environment? Contact me at pm.minimalist@gmail.com or go to the link above to learn more about my custom, on-site workshops.

Made in the USA
Charleston, SC
20 September 2011